HONORING THOSE WHO HONOR

Since 1979, military veterans have come to say farewell to deceased former members of the armed services at Fort Snelling National Cemetery. They are the **Memorial Rifle Squad.** This all-volunteer group has been present at each of the 74,000 funerals conducted at the cemetery for those families that have requested an honor guard. This fraternity has given the final tribute in this manner for the past 38 years, serving up to 17 funerals a day—even in stifling heat and humidity or bone-chilling cold and wind. It seems only fitting that these dedicated people are now honored themselves. They have demonstrated to Minnesotans and all Americans that service to country does not end with the culmination of active duty. The time has come to salute the heroes who honor our heroes buried on sacred ground.

"The dedication that men and women make in order to serve in the armed forces goes well beyond the characteristics of loyalty, duty, integrity, and courage. In Honoring Those Who Honor *author Jim Hoey conveys those grand attributes so prevalent in these former service members. Theirs is a magnificent display of affection and respect as these final honors richly mark the lives and military careers of veterans who have offered their last full measure of devotion."*

— John Forrette,
Colonel, U.S. Army Reserve (Retired) (1982–2012)

"Quietly, without fanfare, notoriety, or payment – the Fort Snelling Memorial Rifle Squad dutifully carries out its solemn task of providing a last final salute to our nation's veterans. They consider it a deep honor to be able to serve our country in this humble capacity. Jim Hoey's book offers a unique and private look at some of the threads in the fabric of what makes America truly great. The precise execution of their honor ritual puts chills down my spine, swells my heart, and chokes me to tears every time I witness it. They are the best of the best and shining examples of selfless sacrifice."

— John Knapp, Deputy Director of
Fort Snelling National Cemetery, Minneapolis, MN

Steve –
Hoping you find this book both interesting
and informative. The rifle squad is a truly
outstanding contingent of selfless veterans.

Warm regards,
Jim
11/10/17

HONORING
THOSE WHO
HONOR

Memorial Rifle Squad –
Fort Snelling National
Cemetery

Jim Hoey

Jim Hoey

NODIN PRESS

ACKNOWLEDGMENTS

I would like to thank all of the people who have supported my efforts in compiling this book and those who gave me suggestions and counsel, especially the dedicated members of the Memorial Rifle Squad at Fort Snelling National Cemetery and specifically to founder George J. Weiss, Jr., historian Jim Jore, past Commanders Terri Winter, Richard Geis, and Mike Pluta, present Commander Allan Johnson, and Fort Snelling National Cemetery Deputy Director John Knapp, who have been so invaluable to this effort. Kudos, also, to all of the people who have shared their stories of loved ones who were buried at Fort Snelling and to all of the volunteers who make Fort Snelling National Cemetery a national treasure.

Thanks to my publisher, Norton Stillman, for his guidance on our fifth book together, and to John Toren for his continued expert work doing layout and final editing. To my buddy and cover artist Paul Roff, what a treat to collaborate on our third book as you evoked the essence of the rifle squad with your splendid artistry. A special thank you to my friend Tom Novitzki, for his ardent support and counsel. I am humbled and truly honored to have had the chance to work on such a project and sincerely hope that others will emulate the patriotism, service, and commitment of this noteworthy group.

ISBN: 978-1-947237-01-8

Library of Congress Cataloging-in-Publication Data
Names: Hoey, Jim, author.
Title: Honoring those who honor : Memorial Rifle Squad - Fort Snelling
   National Cemetery / Jim Hoey.
Other titles: Memorial Rifle Squad - Fort Snelling National Cemetery
Description: Minneapolis, MN : Nodin Press, [2017]
Identifiers: LCCN 2017042788 | ISBN 9781947237018
Subjects: LCSH: Fort Snelling National Cemetery (Fort Snelling, Minn.)
   | Memorial Rifle Squad (Organization : Fort Snelling, Minn.) | Military
   funerals--Minnesota--Fort Snelling. | Veterans--Minnesota--Inter-
views. | Fort Snelling (Minn.)--Biography.
Classification: LCC F614.F7 H64 2017 | DDC 977.6/57--dc23
LC record available at https://lccn.loc.gov/2017042788

Nodin Press
5114 Cedar Lake Road,
Minneapolis, MN 55416

Printed in the USA

In Dedication

To all those who have served in the United States military, past and present, and for all those who have chosen to honor them by recognizing their loyalty and dedication to our nation.

To my 92-year-old father, Edward George Hoey, a U.S. Navy veteran of World War II, who inspired his family and community of Taconite, Minnesota with his service and patriotism through the years.

To my wonderful wife, Ann, thank you for accepting my passion for writing this book and for understanding how important it is to honor these heroes, as well as for your 30 years of serving veterans as a pharmacist at Veterans Affairs Medical Center in Minneapolis.

Contents

Introduction

It was Memorial Day at Fort Snelling National Cemetery—
Monday, May 26, 2014. It always seemed to be a warm day
on that holiday, and this day was typical—it was already 75
degrees and a little humid, and the sun poured down on us as
we sat on folding chairs waiting for the 10:00 a.m. ceremony
to begin. It had become part of our family tradition to attend
Memorial Day services since 2001, when our only child, Eddie,
as a three-year-old, joined my wife, Ann, and me. We had just
moved to her childhood home in Eagan two weeks before, just
across the river from the cemetery and the adjacent airport,
and we had decided that it important for us to show our son an
appreciation for those who had served in our nation's military.
It was and continues to be sobering yet inspiring to be present
on this sacred ground for those festivities.

Unfortunately, Ann was unable to attend in 2014, as she
had to work in her role as a pharmacist at the Veterans Affairs Medical Center, just a mile or two away as a crow flies
on the extreme southeastern border of Minneapolis. She
was in the last of her 30 years serving our veterans there
and was less than two months from retirement. Eddie was
now 16 but didn't flinch when I told him that I was expecting him to join me for the one-hour service. We parked
in the usual spot along LaBelle Drive (named after one of
the eight Medal of Honor winners buried at the cemetery)
and were pleased to see that the cemetery looked absolutely
beautiful as we sauntered along the grave markers towards
the circle where the ceremonies would take place.

Eddie Hoey places flowers at a grave.

As was our custom, we had taken the time to stop by selected graves and pondered their service and life as we perused their personal information on the simple but classy
stone markers. We also presented carnations to individuals
dressed in military uniforms to thank them for their service
and learn a little about their lives. The usual distinguished
guests were present on the raised stage, and the large crowd
was adorned with people wearing the vestiges of past or
present military service.

At 10:00 a.m. sharp, the 34th Infantry Division "Red Bull"
Band and Zurah Pipes and Drums started the musical pre-
lude and the attendees rose as the parade from Mallon Drive
(named after another Medal of Honor recipient) approached
the large gathering. In the lead jeep was the Grand Marshall—George Weiss, Jr. the founder of the Memorial Rifle
Squad at Fort Snelling, the full-time all-volunteer outfit that
conducts military honors at the cemetery. He was driven by
Tom Mullon, who had served for several years as the Director

of the Veteran Affairs Medical Center in Minneapolis and as the president of the Fort Snelling National Cemetery Volunteer Committee. Both men, I would learn, were vital members of the Friday edition of the Memorial Rifle Squad. Behind the lead vehicle were marching former members of the military from past wars, from World War II, Korea, Vietnam, Iraq, and Afghanistan.

Presiding as master of ceremonies was Bob Selden, an Air Force veteran who also served with the Memorial Rifle Squad on Fridays and was the President of the Fort Snelling National Cemetery Volunteer Committee. In perusing the day's program, we saw that the volunteer committee was littered with individuals who served with the cemetery's famed rifle squad.

After the Pledge of Allegiance and the National Anthem, the Armed Forces Salute followed as each of the service anthems were played. Current and former personnel from each of the branches of the military stood for their song as the assemblage cheered. It gave me chills to see these proud men and women accept the recognition from the crowd as the renditions played on. Then, "Anchors Away," that familiar Navy tune, was performed. I thought of my dad, who had been a pharmacist's mate on a hospital ship in the Pacific Theater during World War II.

The distinguished guests were introduced and included Minnesota Senator Amy Klobuchar, who made an impassioned plea in her address in support of the people buried there and those who represent us in the military. No matter one's political motivations, one has to be impressed with Klobuchar's record on veterans' issues and her support of our armed forces. The guest speaker on this occasion was Jim Moffett of the First Minnesota Volunteer Infantry, who gave a sincere speech.

Following a splendid version of "America the Beautiful," a gentleman named Bernie Melter stepped up to deliver the "Gettysburg Address." I had met Melter, a Marine residing in

Roger Otte, a bugler on the Memorial Rifle Squad, sounds "Taps."

Cannon Falls, on previous trips to the event, and I was eager to hear him speak Lincoln's unforgettable words from November 19, 1863. Melter was a proud member of the Lakota tribe and spent years as the president of the Fort Snelling National Cemetery Volunteer Committee. He had served for 22 years as a Gunnery Sergeant and went on to become Commissioner of Veterans Affairs for the state of Minnesota under Governors Arne Carlson and Jesse Ventura. I also recalled Melter being introduced as a member of the Memorial Rifle Squad and I had seen and heard impressive things about that contingent throughout the years.

Bernie read the address slowly but with great conviction and passion, and I was hanging on every word. Fifty years ago my seventh grade history teacher in Bovey, Minnesota, Miss Lavonna Jasper, had our entire class memorize it.

Near the end of the address, I gave my son a friendly slap on the arm and said, "Eddie, I have to write a book on those guys." He said, "What guys?" I answered, "The Memorial Rifle Squad." He nodded and said, "That's a great idea." We smiled broadly as we listened to the benediction. I was fully convinced a few seconds later when the First Minnesota Volunteer Infantry and the Memorial Rifle Squad fired the rifle volley. Of course, to top it off, Robert Pellow and Roger Otte, buglers from the rifle squad, then played an echo rendition of the always melancholy "Taps." I was a bit teary-eyed at that point. Perhaps it was the sentimental and solemn moment—but also the feeling that I would be so privileged to write about such an honorable group. I was committed at that point.

We approached the stage area to greet the dignitaries and deliver more flowers. We thanked the main speaker and met an elderly Navy woman, who was gracious in accepting a peach carnation. We slid over to talk with Bernie Melter, and I told him that I would like to write a book on the rifle squad. He was overjoyed and immediately gave me his contact information. A fellow was undoubtedly in his 90s with a U.S. Army cap was moving his wheelchair near us, and we talked with him about his service in Europe, including D-Day and the Battle of the Bulge.

Most of the crowd had dissipated, and we slowly returned to our vehicle discussing what we should include in the book. Eddie had some good ideas, and we were eager to tell my wife when she returned home that afternoon. While the idea for the book was probably just divine intervention, the seeds of such an endeavor would take decades to develop.

As a boy growing up on the western end of the Mesabi Range in the 1950s and 1960s, in a little iron mining village called Taconite (yes, like the iron ore!), I was surrounded by elements of the military. My maternal grandfather had fought in World War I in France and we had tried on his old uniform many times at his home. Grandma Ethel giggled every time one of the grandkids did it for the first time, no matter the size or age. My father spent three years in the U.S. Navy, and

The Memorial Rifle Squad is photographed at attention at a recent Memorial Day service at Fort Snelling.

several uncles had served in World War II, including Uncle Ken, who won a Silver Star for his service in Italy. Of course, we didn't learn about that until he died decades later because in that era, former military men just didn't speak much about their war experiences.

There was a large board near our village hall in Taconite, right above our outdoor hockey rink, that was a tribute to all the men from town who had served in World War I, World War II, and Korea. Every family, it seemed, had members who performed their service to the country, and our local American Legion club, right across from our hockey rink, was named after two heroes, Whittey and Bennett, who had died in World War I.

The peaceful late 1950s and early 1960s were almost a bucolic time; the economy was booming, families were growing, and life was good. Though we had just two channels on our old Setchell-Carlson black and white TV, every week we could match a movie about World War II heroes. The Fourth of July celebration in Coleraine was something we looked forward to for weeks, and not just for the candy. It was a time to be blatantly patriotic, and what a scene it was to watch those heroes march down the street in their old uniforms, some even from World War I.

As Cub Scouts and Boy Scouts, of course, we learned about the importance of patriotism, and many teachers and staff at our schools were former servicemen. Being in the military was honorable, and it brought prestige. As I became increasingly enamoured of current events, politics, and world geography, I began to develop a more nuanced sense of America's position in the world. But soon the quagmire in Vietnam began to complicate that idyllic view.

By the time I was in eighth grade and had reached the level of Life in Scouts, we were singing Barry Sadler's "Ballad of the Green Beret" at our scout meetings just after witnessing graphic video from the jungles and rice paddies in places we couldn't pronounce on Walter Cronkite's national television broadcast.

Just like Tom Cruise's character, Ron Kovic, in *Born on the Fourth of July*, young males in the country were confronted with a dilemma as the war dragged on and the death count catapulted. We were raised by guys who fought in World War II, and we believed in all those great American traits of manhood—bravery, courage, service, and loyalty. Of course, we wanted to maintain the prevailing "domino theory" of stopping communism. It was the outright evil, right? Now we were being bombarded by radio, television, and newspaper accounts questioning our involvement, and disenchantment was beginning to fester.

Just before my first week of high school at Greenway High School in Coleraine, about 10 of us around the same age camped out in a tent next to my Uncle Slim's house. It was August 1967, and two wars were about the only subject, besides girls, of course, that were being discussed—Vietnam and the Six-Day War between Israel and its Arab neighbors. We might not have all been Rhodes Scholars, but I can vividly recall that each of the guys brought forth some thought-provoking observations. We all wondered which of us would be enlisting and who might even be drafted, if they dare do such a thing. Were one or several of us destined to serve or even die?

In the first month of high school, I became good friends with a girl named Nancy Hermiston. She was a redhead and just a very sweet girl. One day, she was gone from Spanish class. Tragically, her brother Jim had died in Vietnam at the age of 25 as a member of the Air Force. It was a day I won't forget—September 9, 1967. Upon her return to school, I didn't know how to console her. The next spring, a young man from nearby Bovey named Renny Huerd, who was in our town often to visit his cousins, died in Vietnam at age 23.

Renny was buried at Lakeview Cemetery in Coleraine. I was one of the altar boys for his service and stationed at the casket at the burial service. His two young sisters, probably about 10 and 12 years old, were shivering in a brisk wind as a rifle volley pierced the air. The girls, perhaps not expecting it, screamed and shrieked for what seemed like an eternity. To that point in my life, I had never felt so bad for anyone. Their screams became sobs. I remembered the older gents firing their rifles—they were guys I knew from the surrounding town who always marched in the parades. It was first time I had ever witnessed an honor guard. Now the family was being presented the American flag by one of the members of that group. It made an indelible impression on me. As confused as I was about what was happening in Southeast Asia, I was impressed by the honor and integrity displayed by these older fellows.

Our school's hockey team won the state boys' title in mid-February of 1968, at about the same time the Tet offensive was taking root in South Vietnam. Even though it was a military situation we actually won, it turned the face of the war and protesting the war became a tsunami. It was a brutal year— 1968. Martin Luther King and Bobby Kennedy were assassinated. Race riots were rampant, and major cities were burning. That summer of unrest brought news that Calumet's Richie Antonovich, the older brother of my friend and classmate Ron ("Bates"), was killed in action at the tender age of 20. Bates was never the same.

For the remainder of my high school career, there was a drumroll of negativity. A defeatist attitude had engulfed us. The body count mounted. Frustration with the course of the war escalated. Minnesota Senator Hubert Humphrey lost a tight election to Richard Nixon that fall. Negotiations to end the war started, but it wouldn't end for another seven years. It was a political nightmare, to be sure, but it was also splitting families and the social fabric. It was fun being involved with all the excitement of high school activity, but there was always the specter of "'Nam."

Taconite had a few guys who were fighting in Vietnam, guys like Bozy Kyllander and Guy Guyer, and we worried about them and prayed for them. A nationwide draft began in 1969, and all the young men born from 1944 to 1950 were to be in a lottery on December 1. I can recall a big board with 365 numbers listed on it. Balls were fished out of a large circular wire contraption and the date listed on that little sheet of paper was written down. All the young men born on that date would be drafted, unless they had a deferment.

The common view of the high school male population was that someone had to be stupid to consider enlisting. For those who were in danger of being drafted, would they go north to Canada? These types of discussions caused a lot of tension in the homes of proud Americans who had served in earlier times. Deferment? No problem, because attending college was becoming a rite of passage and it qualified you for a deferment, as long as you kept your grades up.

For several years, I had serious thoughts about attending one of the military academies. There was something about their graduates' commitment and loyalty to the nation that I always believed in, and the guys who went there were supposed to be the "best of the best"—all-around guys who were smart, tough, and true leaders. West Point and Air Force both had hockey teams, and I probably could have played for either, but math and science were not my strong suits, and I soon learned that I would have to attend prep school before enrolling. Not interested. I wasn't afraid of the rigid academic and physical standards at the military schools or the military commitment thereafter, but the public's attitude toward the military bothered me. I didn't actively seek a recommendation for entrance into the academies.

Certainly, we had some souls who did enlist and many others who were drafted and served their time. Upon entering college at St. Mary's College in Winona, I was not surprised that there was a lot of animosity and anger directed toward the military and its personnel. Still, I remember being shocked and dismayed when seeing American flags desecrated and the level to which many students were dishonoring our servicemen. Without question, there was a high degree of hostility between those who had opposing viewpoints on our involvement in Vietnam. Those who tried to defend our soldiers, seamen, and airmen, especially those who were drafted and didn't have a choice, were vilified. The music and drug culture added to the consternation, and there was a true generation gap evolving.

In the summer of 1971, I was working as a laborer for Cleveland Cliffs Iron Mining Company at their Hill mine in Calumet. In the midst of doing various jobs in the iron ore operation, I had time to think about the impending draft lottery set for August 5. Dad, who was the manager of the mine, celebrated his

46th birthday that day. Meanwhile, all guys born in 1952 would be following the televised draft lottery. There were several important days to remember, figuring your friends and classmates birth dates. My birthdate, May 14, ended up as draft date #259. At the time, they were taking boys who had numbers up to about 120, or about one-third of all American males born in 1952. I was safe, so to speak. The war continued, and I continuesd to work toward my college degree.

In the midst of all the tension and conflict, there was a magical moment on January 27, 1973. St. Mary's was hosting the Augsburg Auggies in an Minnesota Intercollegiate Athletic Conference hockey tilt at night at our outside rink on campus. We were leading the Auggies 3–1 in the second period, and I was seated on the bench awaiting my shift on the ice. Suddenly, the game came to a halt when our public-address announcer, Jimmy Waldeck, said, "Stop the game, I have an important announcement to make."

He hesitated, and I joked to a teammate that Jimmy must have ran out of vodka and was requesting replenishment. The players and referees on the ice were very confused, wondering what was happening. Standing in the snow at the red line across the rink from our bench, Waldeck then stated, "At this time, I would like to say that in Paris today, Henry Kissinger and Le Duc Tho have negotiated a cease fire to end the war in Vietnam."

We had all known that there were impending peace talks, but the moment took us by surprise. In one of the most curious scenes I have ever witnessed, all the players from both teams and most of the fans joined together on the ice in an impromptu celebration. It was pure unadulterated joy. Everyone in college at that time had friends or family in Vietnam, and now the end could be near. Time stood still. In the midst of this frenzied hug-fest, something caught my eye.

Our bench area was covered by a black tarp, and I could see

a red helmet just above the boards. I skated over to get a closer look and saw Mike Flynn, bent over and staring straight down. "Raisin" was a junior but three years older than us, and he had served a tour in Vietnam. I wondered what was racing through his mind. He never did leave the bench area.

Finally, the game was resumed, but it wasn't the same. Interestingly enough, the aggressiveness of the usual hockey game was absent, as if the teams had come to an agreement to nix any violence or physical provocation. We won 4–1 but the score wasn't important on this night. All of the discussion in our locker room was about the news that the war might be ending. Unfortunately, the ceasefire was violated and the war dragged on for another two years, but still that was a night to remember.

After my sophomore year of college, I was working at a beach owned by Iron Range Township named after my grandpa, Gib Troumbly, the World War I Army Private. I spent considerable time thinking about my quandary while mowing the grass and cleaning the premises. While I was enjoying my classes and playing hockey and the freedom that college offers, I felt tortured. I had seen and witnessed the absolute disdain that many people had for servicemen and servicewomen who had fought or were fighting for the U.S. in Vietnam, and I didn't understand it. Perhaps even worse than that poor treatment was the fact that being a soldier and wearing a uniform became an embarrassment. Guys home on break wouldn't wear their uniforms for fear of rebuke. The guys returning home were ignored, and I could tell that it tore them up. One fellow told me that as soon as he arrived back at the airport from overseas, he raced to the bathroom to change into civilian clothes for fear of any recriminations.

What should I do? I had always thought of joining the military at some point and still had some regret about not attending one of the academies. By July of 1972, things were starting to wind down in Vietnam, but the vitriol against our military was rampant. I drove our blue Chrysler station wagon to Grand Rapids and entered the local recruiting office on Highway 169. After a half-hour or so, the papers to join the U.S. Army Reserve and the officer-training program were in front of me. Pen in hand, I was about to sign the papers, but I didn't.

No one knew about this occurrence and I never discussed it with my parents. Why didn't I sign? Perhaps my disdain for the treatment of our military personnel wasn't reason enough to interrupt my education. After all, it was fun playing college hockey and trekking to Chicago on occasion and having my freedom.

When the war finally ended on April 30, 1975, my angst over the issue of treatment of military personnel didn't ebb. People wanted to forget about the war; they felt it was a bad dream. Meanwhile, the veterans who experienced the war were relegated to the shelf. Most people didn't really know what to do with the drafted and enlisted men who returned home. Not only did the vets have to deal with their own realities of war, but a support system was lacking. The anti-war movement had been successful but what remained was a bizarre fog of uncertainty as to how to integrate the vets back into society.

By the time I was teaching American history and political science in suburban Twin Cities high schools in the late 1970s, a vast majority of the youth did not want to be associated with the military. Any discussion of the recent Vietnam conflagration brought derision and disillusionment. Perhaps at no other time in our history was there less respect or admiration for the armed services and their role. President Reagans two terms in the 1980's helped bring back a semblance of patriotism as America's ambivalence about the military and its view on veterans of the Vietnam conflict started to be tempered.

A seminal point for me came on January 29, 1982. A father of a good friend and hockey teammate, Joe Eckel, had died at

Joe Eckel is pictured at the gravesite of his father, Joseph Eckel, a veteran of World War II.

age 64 and was being buried at 11:30 a.m. at Fort Snelling. Joseph J. Eckel, a Private in the U.S. Army, was wounded in action on a Normandy beach in 1944 and presumably left for dead. He survived a serious head injury and lived another 38 years; he was now being buried in Section W, Site 2276.

On this day, the temperature was -20 with a howling north wind adding to the misery. There was three feet of snow on the ground after a recent storm. Few people had decided to come to the gravesite for the former soldier because of the harsh conditions and the service was brief. I observed an honor guard with several older gentlemen in tow. After the rifle volleys and the playing of "Taps," the small gathering quickly dispersed to the warmth of their cars. As I started the motor in my 1981 Dodge Colt, I watched the van the honor guard was huddled in move to another gravesite not far away and saw the men climb back out.

It dawned on me. This was not an honor guard from Eckel's VFW or American Legion but a unit that volunteered just at Fort Snelling. This group was probably conducting several funerals that day, despite the Arctic conditions. It was 11:45 a.m., and I watched them conduct another honor funeral. Then, sure enough, I watched the van traverse to another section of the cemetery for yet another funeral. Did these guys actually do this all day? This was a special group, indeed!

Meanwhile, the two gulf wars in the Middle East and the attack on 9-11 changed the mind-set of the nation completely around, not about the military's action, but about those who served. It seemed like everybody was jumping on board to support those in the military, and organizations were sprouting up to support veterans and their families like never before. It was becoming commonplace to hear people thanking military personnel for their service; to the Vietnam-era vets, it was a godsend.

Another turning point for me came in 1999 when I transferred to Farmington Middle School West to teach civics to freshmen. Our principal was a dynamic and patriotic 29-year-old named Steven Geis. Equipped with a can-do spirit and the energy of a dozen capable men, Geis was determined to recognize and honor local veterans at the school's annual Veterans' Day celebration. It became the most significant event at the school for a decade and a proud occurrence for the community as a whole. Geis was joined in his effort by Howard Miller, a WWII Army veteran and a member of the Sypal-Lindgren chapter of the Farmington VFW, and the twosome helped created a truly magnificent tribute to former members of the military.

Veterans' Day at FMSW became a highlight for the students and teachers each year. Distinguished leaders graced the podium to give the main address, among them Minnesota Governor Mark Dayton and former Vice President Bob Dole (via phone). After the splendid 90-minute program, the honored servicemen gathered for a catered meal before splitting up into classrooms to speak to the students about their experience in the military. Perhaps this was the most powerful aspect of the day, as students were able to ask questions and the veterans were able to express their appreciation for being recognized. We were so proud of how our students conducted themselves and how much honor they showed the vets, not only in their decorum but in their dress and involvement.

Each year there was a specific group to honor—WWII vets, Korean War vets, Vietnam vets, women in the military, prisoner-of-war survivors, and so on. For the local former vets, men and women, it was a humbling experience and one for which they were extremely grateful. The students learned about commitment, loyalty, and dedication and about appreciating those who have served, no matter the cause. Because of its strong commitment to veterans' causes, Farmington became the first city in the country to be recognized as a Yellow Ribbon Community by the Department of Veterans Affairs.

Geis was no stranger to recognizing the need to appreciate the military. He was a former Cadet Colonel at St. Thomas Academy, and his family volunteers weekly at the Veterans Home in Minneapolis. In 2004, Geis, Miller, and I attended the dedication of the World War II Memorial on the Mall in Washington, D.C., and participated in numerous events that brought recognition to all veterans, including a private meeting with Mr. Dole.

Witnessing how much this outpouring of affection meant to the veterans was powerful. To see hundreds of thousands of former servicemen on the National Mall during President George W. Bush's address was an unforgettable moment. I called Dad to thank him while he was watching the ceremony live back home in northern Minnesota.

In moving so close to Fort Snelling in 2001, it was a no-brainer to decide to attend Memorial Day services at the cemetery each year. We have such fond memories of our youngster commiserating with people like Charles Lindberg, a

Minnesotan who was one of the original "flag-raising" Marines on Iwo Jima, or with dozens of others whom we have met to thank for their service and dedication to the United States.

Over the past 40 years, I have attended numerous military funerals that included an honor guard. They are all to be commended for their dedication and loyalty to those who have served, in whatever capacity. Words cannot describe what it means to those loving family members who receive that American flag from the presenter, who listen to the rifle volleys, and who hear those somber 24 notes of "Taps."

Ann Hoey, a pharmacist at the Veterans Affairs Medical Center and son Eddie visit a gravesite on Memorial Day in 2004.

I feel privileged to have had the opportunity to honor the Memorial Rifle Squad at Fort Snelling National Cemetery with *Honoring Those Who Honor*. I have made dozens of visits to the daily squads over the past two years, and there wasn't a time when I wasn't entertained, enlightened, or inspired. While each squad has its own distinct demeanor and chemistry, there is a decided identity that unites all of the membership. No matter what day of the week, there is one absolute common denominator: once on duty for a service, everyone is reverent.

There was never a time when I wasn't awed by their dedication and resolute loyalty to their cause. When off duty, good humor was a constant and the camaraderie was contagious. They have an undeniable connection, certainly in sharing their active duty experiences but also in their commitment to give honor to the veterans and their spouses at their final resting place. The esprit de corps is evident and there is a true brotherhood among them. I felt it as an outsider, though by the end of my experience with them, they made me feel like I was one of them. I had great respect and admiration for their cause before I started this endeavor and even more for the group and its individuals once it was finished. Best of all, I consider many of them friends today.

The Fort Snelling Memorial Rifle Squad mesmerized me with their myriad of unique personalities and their varied life stories. As dramatically different as they are as individuals, they are united in a common bond to honor those who served and to show respect, appreciation, and sympathy to the living who loved them. To spend time with this incredibly dedicated group has been a true pleasure, and I want to thank each one of them for their infectious enthusiasm, integrity, and blunt honesty. Many of the squad members spoke of the importance of duty when interviewed. Understood. After spending so many hours with the Memorial Rifle Squad at Fort Snelling, it was clear to me, too, that it had become my duty—to bring recognition to them for their laudatory and exemplary service.

HONORING
THOSE WHO
HONOR

Chapter 1

An Idea to Honor

In the fall of 1977, a good friend of former Marine Corporal George John Weiss, Jr., passed away. The friend had been a veteran of WWII and American Legion Post 6690 in Mendota, Minnesota, but that contingent was unable to provide military funeral honors. Weiss, the 4th District Senior Vice Commander for the Veterans of Foreign Wars, was determined to properly honor his buddy, who had served in the Army Air Corps. When the Mendota post asked him if he could arrange a team to salute the friend at Fort Snelling National Cemetery, he received commitments from five other veterans to give tribute to their fallen comrade.

Weiss and his five friends made the best of the situation. There was no special uniform or funeral regimen, just six men honoring a fellow serviceman. Weiss found a high school trumpet player to play "Taps" and paid him $15 for his efforts. Interviewed 38 years later, Weiss said, "We didn't do a very good job, but I knew we could do better, and we certainly left a lot to be improved upon." Thus, an idea was born. Weiss pledged to himself that autumn afternoon that he would establish a memorial squad of former servicemen to honor all the veterans who were to be interred at Fort Snelling, or at least for those families that requested military honors.

That pledge to create a memorial rifle squad wouldn't come to fruition for at least another year, when Weiss retired in October of 1978 after 30 years working at Ford Motor Company in St. Paul as a utility repairman. Weiss started to make presentations at metropolitan American Legion and Veterans of Foreign Wars clubs, urging fellow veterans to join his fledgling organization. He had some general plans, but the main mission was simple—to give American veterans buried at Fort Snelling a proper and respectful military send-off. Weiss was able to convince five other former active servicemen to join him in instituting the project. Interestingly enough, the small group represented each of the four main branches of the service—the Air Force, Army, Navy, and Marine Corps.

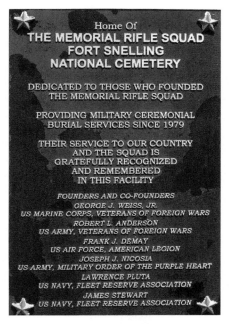

Home Of
**THE MEMORIAL RIFLE SQUAD
FORT SNELLING
NATIONAL CEMETERY**

DEDICATED TO THOSE WHO FOUNDED
THE MEMORIAL RIFLE SQUAD

PROVIDING MILITARY CEREMONIAL
BURIAL SERVICES SINCE 1979

THEIR SERVICE TO OUR COUNTRY
AND THE SQUAD IS
GRATEFULLY RECOGNIZED
AND REMEMBERED
IN THIS FACILITY

FOUNDERS AND CO-FOUNDERS
GEORGE J. WEISS, JR.
US MARINE CORPS, VETERANS OF FOREIGN WARS
ROBERT L. ANDERSON
US ARMY, VETERANS OF FOREIGN WARS
FRANK J. DEMAY
US AIR FORCE, AMERICAN LEGION
JOSEPH J. NICOSIA
US ARMY, MILITARY ORDER OF THE PURPLE HEART
LAWRENCE PLUTA
US NAVY, FLEET RESERVE ASSOCIATION
JAMES STEWART
US NAVY, FLEET RESERVE ASSOCIATION

A plaque honoring the founders of the Memorial Rifle Squad is located at the entrance to the squad room attached to the maintenance facility.

Today, Weiss is the only surviving member of the founding members of the Fort Snelling National Memorial Rifle Squad. When it was formed, George was 50 and the team's youngest member. Weiss was the lone Marine, while Frank J. DeMay was the Air Force representative. Both Robert L. Anderson and Joseph J. Nicosia were U.S. Army vets, and Lawrence Pluta and James Stewart had seen active duty in the U.S. Navy. Weiss remarked, "It was just a coincidence that we had a member from every major branch of the service; it just worked out that way. Every one of those guys was dedicated to making this idea work, and that was our common goal. We weren't in it for the notoriety, we just wanted to serve and do what needed to be done, to give these deceased veterans the respect and honor they deserved for serving our nation."

Early in 1979, the founding group of six met a few times at the Veterans Administration Hospital in Minneapolis to plan their organization and set some ground rules for their operation. Weiss and the others met with the Veterans Administration's Volunteer Services personnel to determine its viability. Further talks then commenced with the Fort Snelling National Cemetery and its director, Doyle Birdshaw. It helped that George was already on the Volunteer Committee for the cemetery. The VA and the cemetery leaders liked Weiss's idea and supported it wholeheartedly. Thus, the Fort Snelling National Memorial Rifle Squad, the first full-time and all-volunteer honor guard at a national cemetery, was created.

"As I was nearing retirement, I was thinking about what I was going to do with all my time," recalled Weiss in early 2015. "I really liked to ride my Harley-Davidson but I couldn't do that year-round in Minnesota. Sure, I would spend some time boating, swimming, and fishing, but it's nice to have a purpose. After working the funeral for my friend from the Mendota post, I was determined to do what I could to give honor to our former serviceman. I felt we owed it to them and their families."

Not that there weren't disagreements over how to proceed with the new outfit. There were many decisions to be made. At the forefront, however, was that the mission was always clear—to honor the veterans and their families with respect and professionalism. Weiss says, "There is no question that we had arguments over how to go about setting up our funeral regimen, but that's because everybody felt so strongly about this project. The big issue is that with guys being from four different branches, each of us had seen military-style funerals and they were all a little different, so we had to compromise. We had high-tempered people, including myself, and we wanted to do the right thing."

"It was a team effort in establishing the rifle squad," continued Weiss. "We all trusted each other, and these guys were people you knew who were committed. When people care that much, there can be differences of opinion about how to progress. We wanted to make this a special organization, especially in an era when service to the country had been so disrespected and ignored. Our group truly wanted to show appreciation for them and their families in their time of need."

Ray Frisvold, who joined the rifle squad in 1979 and became one of the 20 charter members in 1980, says, "The rifle squad was definitely George's brainchild. It was his clear intention to ensure that these deceased veterans would be honored in a dignified manner. He did a lot of work with the various veterans' organizations to make sure we had representation at the original meeting at Fort Snelling to get it established."

By 1978, Minnesota had lost most of its active duty armed forces contingents. In the Twin Cities area, providing military honors at veteran's funerals became nearly impossible—especially at the Fort Snelling National Cemetery. This became more and more apparent as families of veterans began contacting the various congressional officers and the state headquarters of the major veterans' organizations. As the requests increased, it was obvious somebody would have to step forward to establish an organized rifle squad so that traditional military burials could be observed. Thus, George and his cohorts stepped into the void.

In the spring of 1979, more meetings ensued about how to go about formally establishing an organization at Fort Snelling. The organization received endorsement from each of the eight congressionally chartered veteran's groups. General rules of conduct were agreed upon, and it was time to get started. Decisions were made by majority vote and on Tuesday, June 12, the group of six founding members voted in secret ballot to determine which day of the week they would be conducting the weekly funerals. It was determined that Tuesday was the preferred day to

George J. Weiss, Jr, (left) is pictured with fellow Friday squad member Tom Mullon prior to a Memorial Day service in 2015.

work the funeral detail. The first funeral or funerals with a full military honor would be conducted the following Tuesday.

The Tuesday rifle squad had to borrow weapons before they could meet military burial standards. They obtained 10 1903 Springfield rifles from American Legion Post 435 in Richfield. Ideal for close-order drill, the bolt-action, .30 caliber model was perfect for small-arms ceremonial functions, and many of the first volunteers were familiar with them from World War II. Soon, their requests for more rifles led to the U.S. Army relinquishing 35 of them to their care. In 1980, the Army sent them (through the Veterans Administration, at that time) to Fort Snelling and they were all reconditioned and in great shape, according to Weiss.

When first assembled, the Memorial Rifle Squad was housed in a storage area that had once had served as a garage for the cemetery office building. Those quarters featured a wood-burning stove for warming during the cold months and two windows that provided ventilation during hot weather. In

1988, a building once designated as the cemetery director's residence was converted into a conference room, rest rooms for the public, and more spacious headquarters and storage for the rifle squads.

The official name of the contingent is the Memorial Rifle Squad. It has become a model for other national cemeteries. Since the first three funerals on Tuesday, June 19, 1979, the rifle squad has not missed a single military funeral for those families that have requested an honor guard. As of September 1, 2017, the rifle squad had been present at more than 74,000 funerals.

On that first summer day of funerals, the six founders did not have a bugler but used a tape to play the poignant "Taps." Weiss remembered, "We wore out that tape pretty quickly and then we started to get buglers. Our group of six did all the funerals but just on that one day—on Tuesday. At that time, we were doing them only on that day of the week and that was for about two months. As we added more guys, we were able to expand to other days; we needed at least 15 guys, at minimum, to do a creditable job. That first year, I was out here almost every day. "

Weiss added, "The first day of the week we added was Friday. We did that by September that first year, and I became the squad leader for that day. By the fall of 1980, we had added a squad for Thursday, and then Wednesday. Our final day to complete the five-day work-week was the Monday group. So, in a little more than a year, we could now provide a military funeral every day of the week, and that was real gratifying to all of us. We made sure that we would not be shorthanded before moving to a new day. At those meetings, we would then decide who the new squad leader would be for the new day."

Memorial Rifle Squad
Honor Service Start Dates:

Tuesday – June 19, 1979
Friday – September 10, 1979

Thursday – April 3, 1980
Wednesday – September 24, 1980
Monday – February 9, 1981

All it took to add a new day was to have someone suggest that they wanted to create a new squad and to provide enough manpower to handle the minimum requirements for providing a service. Every day was and still is required to provide: Squad leader, bugler, flag folders (2), flag bearers (6), rifle shooters (5–8), and crowd control/car parking (remaining members). An ideal squad requires a minimum of 18 volunteers; however, a full honor service could be done with as few as 11. In the early days, Weiss and the other leaders had to ascertain that they could easily accommodate those funerals until moving on to establish another day. The rifle of use was the pre–World War I rifle, the five-round, bolt-action Springfield M1903 model.

A huge factor in the squad's early years was the support of the Military Order of the Purple Heart (see chapter 5). In the first year, it donated $3,000 for the purchase of uniforms for the new volunteers. For the next 10 years, their backing was critical to the success of the fledgling organization. Weiss says, "If it wasn't for them, we would never have made it."

Transportation to the burial service shelters originally was provided by volunteers using their own vehicles. As the squad for each day began to expand, the procession of squad members sometimes exceeded that of the funeral cortege and delays occurred when moving from one shelter to another. Fort Snelling then provided a van with 10 folding chairs along the sides, but it proved to be problematic, especially when sharp turns or sudden stops were involved. By July of 1980, the State Commander of the Veterans of Foreign Wars, Archie Pavek, provided a used 16-passenger school bus for transporting the rifle squad members.

The "founding six" began to scour veterans' organizations for more members and once they became more visible at

Fort Snelling, the numbers volunteering for the cause began to increase. By the time the squad had approved its charter and passed its constitution and by-laws on January 23, 1980, 20 more members had joined the squad. That group consisted of: Ray Frisvold, Dennis Christy, Bill Weber, Dick Clancy, Anthony Cuff, Russell Green, Carl Falkowski, Dean Hamre, Wallace Herron, Lloyd Isaacson, Lloyd Jackson, Joseph Jasper, James Lang, Alfred Schaeppi, Bob Swanson, Neville Wagoner, Ed Rosander, William Wright, Melvin Schofield, and Glenn O'Malley. The only survivors from that original group are Frisvold, Hamre, and O'Malley. Ray Frisvold, in fact, is still the squad leader for Thursday. Impressively, 10 of the 20 charter members later became the overall Commander for the entire organization.

Weiss worked for Ford at the St. Paul plant after his two-year stint in the Marine Corps ended in June of 1948. Weiss was trained and schooled in the usual locations at both San Diego and Camp Pendleton in California before being dispatched to Guam for a few months. George was a gunner operating a 105 howitzer and 70 years later he can tell you how proficient he was with that apparatus. Weiss was also stationed in other areas in the Pacific Theater after the end of World War II and spent a full year with his forces in northern China.

Born in Newport, Minnesota, on July 6, 1928, Weiss was one of nine children and the oldest boy in his family. His father worked at Cudahy's meat-packing plant in South St. Paul. The Weiss family lived on the east side of St. Paul and young George played some B-squad football and hockey for the Knights of Harding High. He was slated to graduate in 1946. However, Weiss dropped out of school as a 17-year-old senior and enlisted in the Marine Corps on February 6, 1946. He considers the date he joined the Marines as his second birthday, so devoted is he to the Corps to this day. The slender St. Paulite had tried to join a year earlier but was told that he couldn't be sent overseas at that age so he had to wait.

A few days after leaving the hospital in late January of 2015, Weiss was interviewed at his daughter's home. It was a Monday, and though he was still feeling the after-effects of his recent illness, the Marine was determined to be at Fort Snelling to continue his duty as the Friday squad leader four days later. His daughter, Mary Erickson, remarked, "He'll be there; the rifle squad is what he lives for." Despite Weiss's rail-thin appearance, the interviewer that day could see the rough-hewn jaw and the determination of a tiger. Frail from his recent bout with illness, he would still be no bargain in a brawl, even at his advanced age and health status.

George Weiss, no doubt, was and is a no-nonsense kind of guy. He is proud to have been the founder of this highly acclaimed organization and yet humble enough to say that he is just doing what needs to be done. He is a member of VFW Post 1782 in White Bear Lake and the Past Commander of VFW Post 1635 on Payne Avenue in St. Paul. Weiss is still a member of the Marine Corps League, an organization for which he was State Commander for several years. George was on a district draft board that represented parts of five states, including Minnesota, for more than 25 years; he still supports compulsory military service.

Weiss lived in Marine on St. Croix for 61 years and has spent plenty of hours at nearby Big Marine Lake. Any wonder why the guy still considers his greatest legacy that of being a Marine? It was just meant to be. His wife, Bernadine, died in October of 1994. The couple raised five children—son Michael and daughters Mary, Georganne, Cheryl, and Gail. He currently lives with Mary (Erickson) in her home in Maplewood. The proud Marine has 13 grandchildren and eight great-grandchildren. It is clear that his military service is paramount in his life, along with his family.

Mary, obviously dedicated to her father's care and well-being, says, "Dad started the rifle squad when I was 17 years old, and to see it grow into what it is today makes me very proud. It is really impressive to think of what he has accomplished and that he has remained so loyal to this endeavor. He will never give it up. It's a real legacy our whole family shares. His great-grandchildren will be able to say that their great-grandfather started this amazing organization."

George John Weiss, Jr., was honored with the second-highest honor that can be bestowed on an American civilian on August 4, 2010, when President Barack Obama presented him with the Presidential Citizens Medal in a ceremony in the East Room of the White House. Weiss was honored with 12 other Americans that day in tribute to his founding of the Memorial Rifle Squad. The award has been conferred upon extraordinary citizens since 1969, when President Richard Nixon created it.

At the time, the Fort Snelling squads that Weiss helped create had served for more than three decades and for more than 56,000 funerals, never missing a one. Unlike any of the other award winners, he was the lone former serviceman. Prior to receiving the award, Weiss asked a Marine Captain present for the ceremony if he could salute the President. The Captain said," Certainly, after all, he is the Commander-in-Chief." Weiss recalled, "Even though I was now a civilian, I still consider myself a Marine, but I knew that we weren't supposed to salute indoors. It just felt like the right thing to do so after he awarded me the medal, I saluted him. He saluted me right back and it was real snappy, too."

Ted Nemzek, a member of the Friday squad that Weiss has led since 1998, nominated Weiss for the honor and accompanied him to Washington, D.C. Nemzek, a U.S. Army veteran, had volunteered alongside Weiss since 1998. Nemzek remarks, "George is just a hell of a guy; you have to get to know him well to know how incredibly loyal he is to the rifle squads and to the Marine Corps and to his friends. I have written letters to presidents in the past, and I knew former Congressman Al Quie; and he was very helpful in moving his recognition along. George's honor was truly well-deserved."

George Weiss with President Barack Obama at the White House on August 4, 2010, when Weiss was awarded the Presidential Citizens Medal for his work as founder of the Memorial Rifle Squad

Two of Weiss's daughters, Mary and Cheryl, also attended the function at the White House. Weiss was 82 years old at the time but still looked like he could hack basic training. He found about the award in somewhat of a backward fashion.

Months prior to the award ceremony, he received a call from a White House staffer telling him that he would be sent official mail that he was to complete. He said:

I didn't quite know what it was all about. A few days later, I got a FedEx package and there were a lot of papers to fill out, including information regarding an FBI background check. That's how I found out, in their official letter to me. What can I say, here is a kid from the east side of St. Paul being honored at the White House! It was a humbling experience and I was so proud to represent our rifle squads.

It was President Obama's 50th birthday the day I received my award and I got to visit very briefly with him prior to the formal ceremony. I was the final one of the 13 to be recognized and after the salute, I was about to turn and go back to my seat but he grabbed my arm and said, "Good job." Now, that was something. I never expected to be honored in such a way. I was just doing something I liked to do. Unfortunately, somebody has to die for me to do my job.

George Weiss (left) is pictured with Mike Pluta in 2017. Pluta's father, Lawrence, was one of the six founding members of the rifle squad in 1979.

In a 2007 interview for a veterans' organization, Weiss had stated, "I insist on conducting each memorial service the same, with the utmost dignity for the deceased, as if the deceased veteran were a member of my own family. We're out there to do what we all consider important: to take care of our own."

In 2001, Weiss was the focal point of a feature story on WCCO-TV entitled "The Friday Squad." Being the squad leader, he was quoted and filmed extensively and appropriately so, as the rifle squad's founder. News photographer and script writer Tom Aviles was awarded a national Emmy award for the 14-minute clip.

"We don't know 99% of the people we're burying, they are strangers," added Weiss. "But we've all been in the military, and we are just taking care of each other. Some people have said that I try to run my Friday squad like I'm still in the Marine Corps. Well, I'm a Marine and I'm a hard nose, and when

I hear that, I consider it a compliment because these deceased veterans and their families deserve the best."

A member of the Friday squad for 31 years with Weiss, Marine Kevin Burns, states, "George is supremely dedicated and very strict; his commands are always very clear and concise. He has a great delivery in what he wants and he means it when he gives you an order. He's still a Marine, and he runs his team like one. While he's still a Marine at work, at a party or gathering, he's a gentleman. He deserves all the recognition he can get for starting this organization and helping establish what it is today."

Mike Pluta, whose father was one of the founding members, has served on the Friday squad since 2011. On a late February day, he sits in the squad room, clearly moved when queried about what George Weiss brings to the rifle squad. The 69-year-old tells me, "I have the utmost respect and admiration for the man. These guys have no idea what it will be like when he's no longer out here with us. He has really replaced my dad in many ways—they were out of the same mold. George is certainly direct and he is assertive, but above all, he is and remains a Marine, through and through."

"Nobody can question his dedication to the rifle squad," continues a teary-eyed Pluta. "He knows the rules and regulations and the procedures of the rifle squad by heart, and his heart is bigger than he shows outwardly. George has treated me like gold, and I'll never forget that."

Perhaps the greatest compliment that can be paid to George Weiss and his legacy is this: the Fort Snelling Memorial Rifle Squad has never missed a scheduled service for any reason, including inclement Minnesota weather.

Through stealth, the author later uncovered another gem about this proud soldier. As is customary regarding almost nearly every member of the Memorial Rifle Squad, they leave the own plaudits for others to disseminate. Despite numerous opportunities to "blow their own horn," so to speak, they refrain from claiming any personal recognition and honor. Such is also the case with George J. Weiss. One of the Friday squad members approached me in the squad room prior to the day's set of funerals and said, "Do you want to know how dedicated George is to this rifle squad?" "Of course," I uttered, imagining it would certainly be worth relating in the book.

George and the other 12 people who were honored as Presidential Citizens Medal winners in 2010 were to be treated to a whirlwind tour of the D.C. area and VIP treatment on the day after the White House service. The event at 1600 Pennsylvania Avenue took place on a Thursday. George let the authorities in charge know that he would not be attending the first-class functions, the fine dining and the rest. Weiss had to get back to Minnesota on Thursday night. Apparently, he was the only one of the honorees who didn't take part in this opportunity to live the life of a mega-star.

No, George J. Weiss flew back to Minnesota that night and was back in the squad room at Fort Snelling the following morning at 6:30. When I was told that story, I was temporarily stunned. This man was the real thing! A few words entered my consciousness—duty, commitment, service, humility, loyalty. Yes, this tough and demanding fellow truly wasn't just about himself. He lived out his mission in the midst of a time when he could have been soaking in the adulation and the comforts of recognition in the nation's capital. Certainly, he could have taken a day to revel in all his accomplishments and in his squads' successes. No one would have begrudged him that. Wouldn't most of us have taken in all the glory and homage and shared in the so-called "fruits of victory"?

My admiration for the man was already strong, but it was now solidified. Others in the Friday squad were well aware, of course, of that simple act of dedication. When asked about showing up for duty on that day, Weiss retorted, "It was no big deal—I have a duty and I did it. I received my award on behalf of the rifle squad, and it was nice, but there was no question about getting back to what we do." He gave me a look like he might have been insulted at the suggestion that he would have stuck around to take in all the laurels and not shown up for Friday duty. It made me admire him more. My first instinct was to salute him. I did, but only in my mind. After all, George knew I was never in the military.

Still vital at age 89 and as feisty as ever, George J. Weiss, Jr., stands as a living testament to the organization he founded. As proud as he is of its legacy, he knows he's just part of a team. "I had the idea for this outfit, but I had a lot of help putting it together," remarks George on a hot and humid summer day in 2017. "It was like putting together a jig-saw puzzle, and we got it done, piece by piece. It is a group built on dependability, consistency, and professionalism."

On a day when there will be 15 funerals on a steamy summer morning, Weiss stands tall to be introduced to new cemetery director Ame Callahan, who tells him that she heard about their stellar recognition years ago in the Air Force and is looking forward to working with him and the squad. As the squad marches out the squad room toward the bus, George retorts, "It's our job. It's what we do and, hopefully, we do it well."

There is no need to ask Weiss where he will be buried someday. When I relay that thought to him, he quickly shoots back with authority, "Yup, I'll definitely be buried out here, on a Friday, and my urn will be a 105-howitzer shell." Was there any doubt?

Chapter 2

Rifle Squad Organization

The Memorial Rifle Squad was incorporated on August 7, 1982. At the same time, a constitution and by-laws for operation were established. The official name of the group became the Memorial Rifle Squad. It is a civilian organization, not a military configuration, and membership in it does not affect or increase liability for military service. The organization is almost totally self-financed. The U.S. Army provides the shells for the rifles but, otherwise, funding for all they do is done on their own. The Army also supplied the Springfield 1903 model rifles for use for the three-volley salutes used during the honor service.

The Memorial Rifle Squad is a tax-exempt 501c(3) organization, with all its operations and equipment paid for with public donations. There are no benefits or compensation received for any individual on the squad. All members are volunteers providing their time and weekly travel to and from Fort Snelling National Cemetery at their own expense. The squad's main expense is the purchase and operation of the van, which is used primarily to move the squads between services and to provide shelter while waiting for the next funeral. The latest model, a Ford, was purchased in 2014 and seats 26.

Expenses also include squad members' uniforms, rifles, flags, maintenance costs, and miscellaneous supplies. Fort

The van for the Memorial Rifle Squad in front of the squad room attached to the maintenance facility at Fort Snelling

Snelling provides a squad room for the exclusive use of the squad for assembly, meetings, and equipment storage. The nearby Veterans Affairs Medical Center cafeteria provides daily lunches for squad members. Flags are ordered by the quartermaster from a manufacturer in Miami, Florida, and they are 100% cotton. The Memorial Rifle Squad provides a flag for each service, whether or not the funeral home has brought one.

Its Articles of Incorporation (Article 2, Sec. A1) state that the primary purpose for its existence shall be: Fraternal, patriotic, historical, and educational; to perpetuate the memory and history of our dead and promote and preserve any project or equipment relevant to the enrichment of providing Military Ritualistic Honors at Funerals held at Fort Snelling National Cemetery; to maintain true allegiance to the Government of the United States of America, and fidelity to its Constitution and laws; to foster true patriotism and to maintain and extend the institutions of American freedom.

The principal duty performed, or the primary mission of the Memorial Rifle Squad, is to provide a military ceremonial burial service, at no charge, for the family of an honorably discharged veteran. The service will be provided only if requested by the family or a designated funeral director. Any unit of a veterans' organization wishing to participate may be assisted by the Memorial Rifle Squad.

Presently, under the most recent by-laws established in 2007 and reviewed in 2012 and July 2017, the following are the requirements to become a volunteer member of the Memorial Rifle Squad.

The person must be a veteran with an honorable discharge from active military service or currently on active duty (Reserve or National Guard); U.S. Army, U.S. Navy, U.S. Air Force, Marine Corps, Coast Guard, et al.

The person must be a member of a Veterans' Service Organization. Most belong to an American Legion club, a Veterans of Foreign Wars club, Disabled American Veterans, or Military Order of the Purple Heart.

The person must submit a Form DD214 (Discharge Papers and Separation Documents) to the squad leader and obtain an approved identification badge from the Veterans Administration Medical Center, Volunteer Services

The main officer of the Memorial Rifle Squad is the Commander, who is elected at the annual meeting held in early January and serves for the next calendar year, as does the Vice Commander. The Commander is elected by the membership, as are all the other main officers. In early spring, the entire rifle squad gathers for a formal dinner and installation of officers. In December, each of the daily squads elects its own Squad Leader and Assistant Squad Leader(s).

Officers for 2017:
Commander: Allan J. Johnson
Vice Commander: Daniel D. Kirchoffner
Adjutant: Tom H. Osborne
Finance Officer: Theresa A. Winter
Quartermaster: Richard D. Asbury
Assistant Quartermaster: Gary L. Klein

Chaplain: Daniel D. Kirchoffner
Historian: James R. Jore
Chief Medical Officer: Richard R. Zech
Trustees: Michael L. Pluta, Robert H. Nelson, Richard T.
Geis
Officer of the Day: Kenneth W. Gibson, Jr.
Ordnance Officer: Howard R. Tellin
Assistant Ordnance Officer: Leo E. Noe
Squad Leaders: Monday – Mike Rose
Tuesday – Daniel J. Fisher
Wednesday – Leo E. Noe
Thursday – Raymond V. Frisvold
Friday – George J. Weiss

Prospective members are asked to visit the Memorial Rifle Squad on the day on which they wish to volunteer and to spend at least two days observing the group and familiarizing themselves with the proceedings. That day's squad will then determine whether or not to welcome the candidate as a member of the squad. The new member is also required to register with the Voluntary Services Office at the Minneapolis Veterans Affairs Medical Center.

The new volunteer is issued a purchase order for issuance of uniform trousers (black) and shirts (white) and is issued other standard garb: caps with emblems (black), ties (black), tie clasp (gold, with 35-year pin attached), belts and buckle (black), winter jacket (black), spring or summer jacket (black), duty belt (white), and gloves (white). Collar pins with the Memorial Rifle Squad insignia are also issued and are regularly worn by all the members. Issuance of the uniform is the responsibility of the quartermaster, Rich Asbury, who has been in that position for the past 15 years.

Uniforms are worn with issued caps and emblems (winter); jackets (no additions); shirts (no additions); ties, with tie

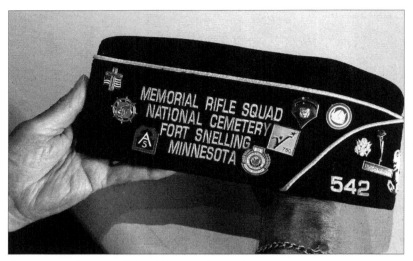

A cap worn by one of the rifle squad members

bars optional; belts; and trousers. Individual veterans' overseas organizational caps may be worn at the member's prerogative and may include a variety of military pins. Many of the caps worn by squad members are either from local VFW or Legion Posts and are usually spiced with interesting pins that depict their branch of service and maybe their division.

Uniforms may be worn only at Fort Snelling National Cemetery and veterans' organizational meetings or such meetings that are beneficial to the rifle squad. They shall never be worn at any political function, or any activity whatsoever, that infers endorsement of the Memorial Rifle Squad. White shirt sleeves with open collars are utilized officially from May 1 through September 30, and a summer jacket is optional, depending on the weather conditions. Heavy black parkas and trooper caps are worn during the frigid months, and raincoats are available. During winter, members furnish their own undergarments. In all of my visits to the services at Fort Snelling, I have never witnessed an outfit that was not uniform, so to speak.

There are certain unofficial standards for membership on the Memorial Rifle Squad. Generally, it is expected that each member be available for 45 weeks, except for reasonable absences. New candidates must meet with the day's squad leader to determine their interest and dedication level and agree to maintain their uniform in a clean and presentable manner. New members provide their own thermal wear, socks, and blacks shoes or boots. Of course, they must agree to abide by the constitution and by-laws of the rifle squad. Once established on a certain squad, a transfer to another day can be made based on need and acceptance of the current members of each squad.

Careful attention is made to care for the rifles used by the Memorial Rifle Squad. The riflemen who are to fire the volleys for the day's funerals take the responsibility to clean their weapon before use. The Army-issued rifles are 1903 or 1903A Springfield bolt-action weapons. The models predate World War I and were the standard infantry rifle used by the military for decades before being replaced by the M-1 Garand just prior to World War II.

Unfortunately, a major controversy surrounding the Springfield rifles occurred in late 2011. A new policy was developed by the Army that would force the rifle squads to use the semi-automatic M-1 and discard their Springfields. The directive would not only force them to change rifles but would limit them to using just 15 of the new version and to less ammunition also. The goal was to give groups a more modern weapon but the Memorial Rifle Squad became unified in opposition to the change. Artis Parker, the director at Fort Snelling at the time, was a strong advocate for the rifle squad maintaining the status quo with the rifles and gave strong support to their cause.

Bob Nelson, a member of the Wednesday squad, remarks, "Guys like the Springfield because it is much safer and easier to operate. It has a distinctive ring to it, too, and it just sounds better. It is easier to clean and has less maintenance. Also, the M-1 can hurt you because the 'thumb' is a big problem. When you go to push a clip of shells into the rifle, it releases the bolt to slam a shell into the gun's breech, and you can get your thumb smashed if you don't release it quick enough."

The 1903 Springfield models were popular for groups like the American Legion, Veterans of Foreign Wars, Disabled American Veterans, and others who had used them for ceremonial purposes for many years. Former veterans involved with honor guards and rifle squads who used them enjoyed their simplicity and their unique and mellow sound. The Springfield rifle was produced 1903–49 by the Springfield, Massachusetts, armory, which was federally-owned. They weigh 8.7 pounds and are 43.2 inches long. The feed system is a five-round clip.

Squad members were adamant about not wanting to change their rifles. To them, the Springfields were efficient to maintain and possessed the proper sound that is so key to their ceremonial rifle volleys. Howard Tellin, another Wednesday member who is the ordnance officer for the Memorial Rifle Squad, said, "We weren't happy that some guy with the Army was trying to make his mark with some new

Howard Tellin, a member of the Wednesday squad and the chief ordnance officer, is pictured with a 1903 Springfield rifle, the weapon used for the rifle volleys at Fort Snelling.

policy to take our rifles away. The Springfield is a simple weapon with only seven movable parts, and the two models we use have interchangeable parts, which makes them easy to maintain."

While the Memorial Rifle Squad marshalled together in defiance of the new order, a former Marine got intertwined in the conflict. John Kline, the Second District Congressman from Minnesota, went to work on the political scene. It helped that Kline was serving on the Armed Services Committee in the U.S. House of Representatives at the time. Kline sent a letter to Army Secretary John McHugh asking for reconsideration of the new policy.

In February of 2012, in a reversal of the directive a few months earlier, the U.S. Army would allow the Memorial Rifle Squad to retain the favored 1903 Springfield rifles that were issued to them back in 1980. Following the Army's decision, Kline announced the introduction of "Honoring Our Nation's Outstanding Rifle Squads," a bill that would allow the Secretary of the Army to loan or donate more than 15 excess rifles to eligible organizations like the Memorial Rifle Squad.

Currently, the rifle squad has 40 rifles that are used weekly and several others that are used for spare parts. Ten are used on a daily basis, with eight actually firing and two serving as ceremonial (chrome) rifles. Some gun experts consider the 1903 Springfield model to be the best bolt-action rifle ever— dependable and tough. I will add that it has a cool design, a nifty finish, and nice balance as you hold it in your hands. The issue with the ammunition was resolved, and the squad receives a palate of blank shells every three months from an Army base in Missouri. The shells, incidentally, are crimped at the top but do contain some gunpowder, resulting in their unique sound. Annually, the Memorial Rifle Squad fires approximately 54,000 rounds, a testament to the efficiency of the 1903 Springfield.

"The guys were very relieved when the issue was settled and common sense prevailed," says Nelson, five years after the controversy was settled. "I was Commander at the time, and it was a huge hassle; we are just happy it ended the way it did." Despite the anxiety the issue created for the rifle squad, it is still clearly evident that it brought the squads closer together and brought more recognition to their cause.

MEMBERSHIP INFORMATION

Currently, members are drawn from the American Legion, American Veterans (AmVets), Disabled American Veterans, Ex-Prisoners of War, Korean War Veterans, Marine Corps League, Military Order of the Purple Heart, Fleet Reserve Association, First Marine Division Association, Veterans of Foreign Wars, and the Vietnam Veterans of America.

As of mid-2017, there are 129 certified and active members of the five daily squads. Three gentlemen (Allan Johnson, Ken Gibson, and Andy Urness) serve two days a week and are counted twice. All but one of the volunteers is a male; former Army reservist Terri A. Winter is the only woman on the overall squad and serves on Wednesdays. There are 26 members on the Monday and Wednesday squads, 25 on the Tuesday and Thursday squads, and 27 on Friday. There are 101 former

Commander Allan Johnson (left), Ken Gibson (middle), and Andy Urness (right) are pictured prior to Monday's services. They are the only three current members who serve two days a week. Johnson also serves on Thursdays while Urness and Gibson volunteer on Friday.

members who are officially regarded as inactive. As of September 1, 2017, there are 194 deceased members who have served since the inception in 1979. All told, 420 persons have been official members of the Memorial Rifle Squad. (Note: A full list of the inactive and deceased members can be found in the addendum in the back of the book.)

As of mid-2017, the average age of a member of the rifle squads was 74. However, with the demise of the World War II era member, the age is lowering. Each year, the five squads that make up the Memorial Rifle Squad log more than 40,000 volunteer hours and drive more than 175,000 miles to travel to Fort Snelling National Cemetery to do their service. In a review of the attendance over the years, it is apparent that the volunteers take their obligation seriously. When members are absent, it is usually for a significant reason—injury, illness, or an important family matter. The status of whether a member is an active or inactive member is made by that day's squad leader.

Regarding longevity, 13 members of the current active squad have served at least 20 years, led by founder George J. Weiss, who is now in his 39th year of service. Thursday squad leader Ray Frisvold has the second-longest tenure with 38 years. Friday volunteer Charlie Korlath, who has presented the flag to approximately 19,000 families himself, has 36 years on the squad. Gordy Carlson of the Wednesday squad has volunteered for 33 years. Another Friday squad member, Edward (Kevin) Burns, has served 31 years.

Meanwhile, two other Friday squad volunteers have at least 20 years—Ted Nemzek (20) and Andy Urness (26), who also serves on Mondays. On Wednesdays, squad leader Leo Noe (23), Rich Asbury (23), Howard Tellin (21), and Clarence Dick (20) all have surpassed that mark. Bob Pellow, a bugler on Mondays, has served 27 years.

Glenn O'Malley, the youngest of all the members to first join the rifle squad in 1979, and the 17th Commander in 1997, served for 31 years. He is the longest-serving inactive member after culminating his duties in 2010. Glenn volunteered on Tuesdays and Fridays before spending most of his tenure with the Monday squad. Other inactive members who have volunteered at least 20 years include: Kermit Bischoff (20 on Tuesday), Martin Pavek

(21 on Tuesday) Leon Simon (23 on Tuesday), Clarence Kraemer (24 years with Tuesday and Thursday), Harold Brick (20 on Thursday), and August Joubert (24 on Thursday).

Deceased members with a minimum of 20 years include: Richard Clancy (20 on Thursday), Robert Swanson (20 on Friday), John O'Neill (21 on Monday), Philip Carney (22 on Monday), Lester Durose (23 on Tuesday), James Lang (23 on Thursday and Friday), Albert Lavansky (23 on Tuesday and Thursday), Walter Mickelson (24 on Monday), Dennis Christy (27 on Monday), and Wallace Herron (27 on Tuesday).

Ray Frisvold, the squad leader on Thursdays, is photographed in the squad room prior to honor services in August of 2017. Frisvold joined the rifle squad in its first year (1979).

Regarding the years when current members joined, two joined before 1980, two joined from 1980 up to '85, two joined from 1985 up to 1990, three from 1990 up to '95, six from 1995 up to 2000, 18 from 1995 up to 2000, 43 from 2005 up to 2010, 36 from 2010 up to 2015, and 13 from 20015 through 2017.

As for the make-up of the squads based on branch of service midway through 2017, the U.S. Army leads with 60 of the 129 members. With nearly half of the squad (47%), Army veterans make up at least half of the squads on Tuesday, Wednesday, and Thursday. They are a majority on every day of the week, a fact that often gets discussed in the friendly banter regarding service superiority. The U.S. Navy has the second-largest contingent with 34 squad members (26%). The Marine Corps is next with 23 current members (18%). The Air Force has 11 former veterans (9%), including five on Wednesday. The Coast Guard has one member, Robert (Joe) Johansen, who serves on Thursdays.

Chapter 3

Burial Procedures, Arrangements, Eligibility

The Memorial Rifle Squad has long had specific procedures for how they provide for a military burial service at Fort Snelling. The hierarchy has continually updated its manual of procedures for the membership. After there were significant enough numbers, a team was created for each day of the week, led by a squad leader. Thus, each member of the Memorial Rifle Squad is assigned to a team for Monday, Tuesday, Wednesday, Thursday, or Friday.

There are approximately 24–26 volunteer members on each squad, and there is usually a minimum of 21 volunteer–members present for each service. The busiest day for funerals, as charted by historian Jim Jore, is Friday, with Monday the next busiest day. Tuesday, Wednesday, and Thursday are generally less busy but usually average around the same number yearly. While the cemetery averages 5,300 burials a year, the Memorial Rifle Squad averaged approximately 2,500 services each year during the past decade. Through the first half of 2017, they were on pace to set a yearly mark for the most honor services.

Each new member of the Memorial Rifle Squad is given a manual that cites the constitution, by-laws, and the procedures for performing their service. While the procedures are recommended, there is little if any discrepancy in the operations from day to day between the five different squads. The last time the procedures were revised was in July of 2017 when Commander Allan Johnson led a team with former Commanders Mike Pluta (2016), Terri Winter (2014) and Richard Geis (2015), and Tuesday squad leader Dan Fisher.

Burial Arrangements

The funeral home or next-of-kin makes contact with the National Cemetery Scheduling Office to make burial arrangements for veterans, spouses, and/or eligible dependents. The funeral home can fax all available military discharge documents to the scheduling office (866) 900-6417 (fax) or scan and e-mail documentation to *NCA.Scheduling@va.gov* with the name of the decedent in the subject line. Follow up with a call to (800) 535-1117 to schedule the internment. If military discharge documents are not available, a scheduling office representative can assist the funeral home or next-of-kin with the verification process. Requests for eligibility determination when no military discharge documents are available may require 48 hours or more for verification.

Persons Eligible for Burial
in a National Cemetery

The National Cemetery Scheduling Office has the primary responsibility for burial in Veterans Administration National Cemeteries. A determination of eligibility is made in response to a request for burial in a VA national cemetery.

A) Veterans and Members of the Armed Forces (Army, Navy, Air Force, Marine Corps, Coast Guard):

1 - Any member of the Armed Forces of the United States who dies on active duty.

2 - Any veteran who was discharged honorably.

3 - Any citizen of the U.S. who, during any war in which the

United States has or may be engaged, served in the Armed Forces of any government allied with the U.S. during that war, who was terminated honorably by death or otherwise, and who was a citizen of the U.S. at the time of entry into such service at death.

B) Members of Reserve Components and Reserve Officers' Training Corps:

1 - Reservists and National Guard members, who at time of death, were entitled to retired pay or would have been entitled, but for being under the age of 60.

2 - Members of reserve components, and members of the Army National Guard or the Air National Guard who die under honorable conditions while performing active duty for training or inactive duty training.

3 - Members of the Reserve Officers' Training Corps of the Army, Navy, or Air Force who die under honorable conditions while attending an authorized training camp or cruise.

4 - Members of reserve components who, during a period of active duty for training, were disabled or died from a disease or injury incurred in line of duty.

C) Public Health Service—a commissioned officer of the Regular or Reserve Corps of the Public Health Service who served on full-time duty on or after July 29, 1945.

D) World War II Merchant Mariners—U.S. Merchant Mariners with ocean-going service during period of armed conflict during that war.

E) The Philippine Armed Forces—any Philippine veteran who was a citizen of the U.S. or who served in the organized military forces of the government of the Philippines from 1945-47.

F) Spouses and Dependents:

1 - The spouse, surviving spouse or dependent of an eligible veteran or member of the Armed Forces may be eligible for interment even if that veteran is not buried or memorialized in a national cemetery.

2 - The surviving spouse of an eligible veteran who had a subsequent remarriage to a non-veteran.

3 - The minor children of an eligible veteran; a minor child is a child who is unmarried and who is under 21 years of age.

G) Parents—biological or adoptive parents whose biological or adoptive child was a service-member.

PERSONS NOT ELIGIBLE FOR BURIAL IN A NATIONAL CEMETERY

Former Spouses—a former spouse of an eligible individual whose marriage to that individual has been terminated by annulment or divorce.

Other Family Members (see above).

Disqualifying Characters of Discharge—a person whose only separation from the Armed Forces was under dishonorable conditions or whose character of service results in a bar to veterans' benefits.

Discharge from Draft—a person who was ordered to report to an induction station, but was not actually inducted into military service.

Individuals Found Guilty of a Capital Crime—interment is prohibited if a person is convicted of a federal or state capital crime, for which a sentence of imprisonment for life or the death penalty may be imposed.

Individuals Convicted of Certain Sex Crimes—interment is prohibited if a person has been convicted of a Tier III sex offense and was sentenced to a minimum of life imprisonment.

Subversive Activities—any person convicted of subversive activities shall have no right to burial in a national cemetery.

The scheduling office is open seven (7) days a week, from 7:00 a.m. to 6:30 p.m., central time, except for Thanksgiving Day, Christmas Day, and New Year's Day. Contact the cemetery directly (612) 726-1127 or fax (612) 725-2059 to:

- schedule memorial services without interment
- cancel or reschedule interments
- change information provided to the scheduling office
- request disinterment or relocation of remains

Burial Benefits

Burial benefits provided by the National Cemetery Association, at no cost to the veteran or his or her family, include: burial plot, opening and closing of the gravesite, a government liner, headstone, or marker with inscription, interment flag, perpetual care of the gravesite, and a Presidential Memorial Certificate. Funeral director's services are not covered, however. There is no waiting list for burial in a VA National Cemetery, and this is the case at Fort Snelling.

Minneapolis has been identified as the 12th coldest city in the United States, but harsh winters do not stop burials at the cemetery. The cemetery each fall prepares approximately 1,000 gravesites by setting blank headstones, preparing in-ground cremation sites with covers, and compacting fall leaves from the adjacent city of Richfield into full-size casket sites. These processes ensure first interments are easily accessible to the veteran and his or her family, despite a very deep frost level in the ground.

The large visual expanse of the cemetery, while awe-inspiring to the public, generally leads to the question of future availability. Considering current and planned rates for all burial types (casket, cremation, and scatter) along with the available developed sites and the future development of existing acreage, the cemetery is expected to remain in operation past the year 2060.

Gravesites are assigned by the cemetery and cannot be selected in advance. Assignments are made without regard to rank, ethnic or religious background, branch of service, or other such factors. The veteran and spouse are interred in the same grave. If both are veterans, they may be buried side-by-side in separate graves. The burial site options include: casket (in-ground only); cremation (in-ground); cremation (above-ground columbarium); and cremation (scatter garden, which is available from April 1 to November 1). To mark the gravesites, the cemetery utilizes upright marble markers, marble niche covers for columbaria and the memorial wall, and flat granite markers for the flat burial sections.

Military honors are provided by the Department of Veterans Affairs, unless provided by the Department of Defense, and are arranged by the funeral director. If there is no funeral director, cemetery staff assist the family in arranging for military honors. Honor guards from local American Legion and Veterans of Foreign Wars organizations, plus the Vietnam Veterans of America, also conduct funerals at Fort Snelling.

Burials and interments are scheduled between 9 a.m. and 2:00 p.m., Monday through Friday, except designated holidays. Upon request, the Memorial Rifle Squad performs funeral honors daily for as many as 17 veterans. No services are scheduled on a Saturday, Sunday, or a federal holiday. Each funeral honor ceremony includes a color guard, a rifle volley, the folding and presentation of the U.S. flag, and a live bugler playing "Taps." Out of respect for all persons buried at the cemetery, the main flag is lowered to half-staff 30 minutes before the first service, where it remains until 30 minutes following the last service of the day.

MILITARY HONOR PROCESS

The squad leader for the day receives a list of funerals for the day from the administration office. It details the name of the deceased, the branch of the military they served in, the committal area the services will be held at, the time of the service, and the funeral home. Services are slated at 15-minute intervals, starting with the top of the hour. Family members and other mourners arrive at Gate 3 and then park on one of six assembly areas. They are met there by a Department of Veterans Affairs employee known as a Cemetery Representative.

The Cemetery Representative leads the funeral entourage to the committal area, where rifle squad members help park the cars and provide security. The Cemetery Representative is the individual who had direct contact with the family and other attendees and is the liaison between the funeral director and the family. The CR stays with the family until the burial detail takes the casket or urn for burial elsewhere in the cemetery. The CR group, which works full-time, includes Karlette Rizzi, Michael Adams, Larry Kozian, Jason Cassellius, Dan Wagner, Kirk Carson, and leader Bob Roeser. Terry Winter, a member of the Wednesday rifle squad, also works part-time for them.

George Gonzalez, who served on the honor guard at Arlington National Cemetery while on active duty, boards the van for Monday services.

In addition, a member of the Fort Snelling Honor Society is present to provide support for the family. Founded in 1991 with the endorsement of General Colin Powell, Chairman of the Joint Chiefs of Staff, the Honor Society is made up of members from the local veterans' organizations and military-affiliated groups, both men and women. Their purpose is to offer condolences and emotional support to the families, and a member is present at services where military honors are requested. The current group includes Sheryl Osburn, Suellen Lindemann, Chrys Holland, Judy Heiser, Chris Drew, and Laurie Pekarik.

After preparing themselves for the days' funerals in their squad room located in the cemetery maintenance facility, the Memorial Rifle Squad leaves approximately 15 minutes before the first scheduled honor service and parks their van adjacent to the committal area. To provide for a proper and dignified military honor for the funerals, recommended procedures have been implemented to make certain there is uniformity in the conduct of their affairs.

The ideal squad for any given day consists of the following:
Squad leader
Two flag folders (one of them will also be presenter of the flag)
Bugler (1 or 2)
Six flag bearers; in order, U.S. flag, Army, Marines, Navy, Air Force, Coast Guard
Rifle squad (6–8) (usually six members)
Chrome rifleman (2, but not shooting)
Color guard leader (usually an assistant squad leader)
Car parkers/security (2)

Thus, a squad requires a minimum of 18 or 19 volunteers, not counting someone allocated to drive the bus. An honor guard, at minimum, requires at least 11 volunteers with a minimum of five riflemen. There is some flexibility in what roles will be utilized depending on the size of the assembly. A small gathering does not require volunteers helping the mourners park their vehicles.

Once directed, the Cemetery Representative leads the entourage to the committal area (there are just three committal areas for casket ceremonies, in addition to the area where the columbarium is located for cremated remains). The lead car, the hearse, and the rest of the vehicles then park three-abreast on the street adjacent to the committal area.

The Wednesday squad assembled at a burial committal area.

By this time, the van utilized by the Memorial Rifle Squad has been parked near the committal area and is in place for the arrival of the mourners. Before the entourage arrives, the Memorial Rifle Squad is already in position for the service. The flag folders take their positions at the entrance of the committal or burial shelter. If the size of the funeral cortege requires assistance in parking cars to prevent delay in providing the military honors and memorial service, the flag folders or the bus driver offer assistance.

The color guard position is opposite the catafalque and the U.S. flag is in direct line to the catafalque. The color guard, of course, is made up of the two chrome riflemen and the six flag bearers. The chrome riflemen are alert to assure that no one

Committal Shelter 2 with a casket on the catafalque

passes between the colors and rifles. Once the casket is removed from the hearse, the color guard and the rifle squad come to attention at the direction of the color guard leader, who is usually either the squad leader or an assistant squad leader.

The rifle squad positions itself behind and to the side of the color guard where it is visible to the mourners in the shelter, yet at a distance that the concussion from the rifle volleys will not be too disturbing to the mourners.

For cremations, the flag is to the right of the remains when the flag folder and presenter escort the remains and the flag to the catafalque. The remains are placed upon the catafalque, and the flag is positioned against the remains container. The flag folder and presenter step back and salute until the service begins.

When the attendees are all arranged inside near the burial shelter, the funeral director acknowledges that the military honors may begin. One of the flag folders, previously designated, salutes the squad leader. The squad leader calls the rifle squad to "Attention." At this command, the flag bearers place the base of the flagpoles in the pocket of their carriers. The squad leader then commands, "Present Arms." At this point, the color guard riflemen come to "Present Arms," and the military flags are dipped or lowered.

Then, the squad leader gives the following commands: "Unlock"; "Ready" (right foot one-step back); "Aim," "Fire." After firing the first volley, the squad leader must be aware that all riflemen are able to clear spent shells and insert another round. If a rifleman is having difficulty with his rifle, he should take the "Ready" position and then simulate firing on the next command. The next command is: "Aim"; "Fire." The riflemen again eject the spent shells and insert another round. The same commands are repeated again and the third volley is fired. This time, however, the riflemen do not eject the spent shells but take the "Ready" position. The squad leader then commands: "Ready Front" and "Present Arms."

There has been much misinformation about a so-called "21 Gun Salute." Firstly, any military serviceman can tell you that a "gun" is always a cannon or howitzer. The only person entitled to a "21 Gun Salute" is the U.S. President. The number "21" comes from the sum of the numbers 1776, of course, the year of the birth of the nation. The Vice President is entitled to a 19-gun salute and some top Generals and Admirals to a 17-gun salute. The so-called "guns" utilized by the Memorial Rifle Squad are 1903 Springfield rifles. The military honors afforded by the rifle squads are actually "three-volley" salutes. If there are six riflemen, then 18 shots will be fired. Even if seven riflemen are present, there are 21 shots fired but it's not considered a salute, simply a three-volley send-off. Immediately after the rifle volleys, the bugler or buglers now sound "Taps," the 24-note melancholy farewell tune.

If there are two buglers, often they play "Echo Taps," a version in which the second bugler follows a few notes behind the first. Following "Taps," if the flag has been folded prior to arriving at the cemetery, the color guard and rifle squad remain at "Present Arms." The bugler, squad leader, and color guard also

The Wednesday rifle squad is about to fire a volley.

continue to render salutes until the flag has been presented to the flag recipient, who is seated at a designated spot so there is no confusion as to who is to accept the flag for the family.

If the flag has not been folded, the command "Order Arms" is given to the color guard and rifle squad and both groups remain at attention. The flag is folded by the two flag folders in its customary 13 folds. When they have completed the folding and the presenter is in possession of the flag, the squad leader commands, "Present Arms."

The present rendition of "taps" is based on a French bugle signal, called "tattoo," that notified soldiers to return to their garrisons for the night. The last five measures of the "tattoo" resemble "Taps." The current revision of "Taps" was made during America's Civil War by Union General Daniel Adams Butterfield. Camped at Harrison Landing, near Richmond, Virginia, Butterfield decided the music was too formal to signal the day's end. One day in July 1862, he recalled the prior version and hummed a version of it to an aide, who wrote it down in music. The brigade bugler, Oliver M. Norton, played the notes and after, listening, Butterfield lengthened and shortened them while keeping his original melody.

Butterfield then ordered Norton to play this new call at the end of each day. The music was heard and appreciated by other brigades, who asked for copies and adopted this bugle call. It was even adopted by Confederate buglers. The music was made the official Army bugle call after the war but was not given the name "Taps" until 1874. "Taps" is now played by the military at burial and memorial services, to accompany the lowering of the flag and to sign the "lights out" command at the end of the day.

Charlie Korlath (right) presents the American flag to Jeff and Kathy Hagen on a Friday in May, 2015 at the service for Jeff's father John.

The presenter, in his most dignified manner, then presents the flag (point side toward himself and the stars up) to whomever is to accept the flag. A blue packet with three spent shells and the rifle squad card are also given to the family at this time. The flag presenter then delivers the presentation speech:

> *On behalf of the President, the Armed Forces of the United States, and a grateful nation, I present you this flag, a symbol of our Great Republic, for which our departed comrade has honorably served.*

When the flag recipient appears to be holding the flag firmly, the presenter steps back one pace and, with the assistant flag folder, renders a hand salute until the command "Color Guard, Port Arms" is given. Both then move out of the shelter, in step. When the flag folders have exited the shelter, the squad leader commands: "Color Guard, Port Arms, right (or left) Face, Forward March." The lead chrome rifleman leads the color guard back to the bus and dismisses them. The rifle squad remains at "Present Arms" until the colors pass by if this is the case. The squad leader then commands to the rifle squad: "Port Arms, right (or left) Face, Forward March." The return to the van is reverentially quiet and respectful. The bugler and flag folders pick up spent shells following the military honors.

FOLDING THE FLAG

There are 13 triangular folds in folding the American flag and a tribute has been designated to each fold.

1) To the symbol of Life

2) The Belief in Eternal Life

3) In Honor and Remembrance of the Deceased Veteran

4) For Divine Guidance

5) In honor of "Our Country"

6) Our Pledge to the Flag

7) Tribute to the Armed Forces

8) To Honor the Mothers of Veterans

9) Tribute to Womanhood, for their faith, love, loyalty, and devotion to Veterans

10) Tribute to the Fathers who have given of their sons and daughters to the Armed Forces

11) In the eyes of the Hebrew citizen, the seals of Kings David and Solomon

12) In the eyes of the Christian citizen represents the Emblem of Eternity

13) Stars are uppermost reminding us of our nation's motto, "In God We Trust"

Note: The triangle-folded flag represents the cocked hat worn by soldiers serving under General George Washington and the sailors and marines serving under Captain John Paul Jones in the Revolutionary War. Also, the flag has 13 alternating stripes (7 red, 6 white) that represent the 13 original colonies/states.

Chapter 4

Fort Snelling National Cemetery

GENERAL INFORMATION

Fort Snelling National Cemetery is part of the National Cemetery Administration under the auspices of the Department of Veterans Affairs. It serves as the official home of the nation's first all-volunteer Memorial Rifle Squad. The area consists of 436.3 acres, making it the 18th largest national cemetery out of 135 in terms of land area. Fort Snelling consistently ranks as the fourth-busiest national cemetery, in terms of the number of annual interments. The cemetery is located at the southernmost border of Minneapolis at 7601 34th Avenue South. It is bordered by I-494 on the south, Minneapolis–St. Paul Airport on the east and north, and to the east by the airport and Highway 5.

Access to the cemetery is via the 34th Avenue exit off of I-494; the main cemetery entrance is the first gate on the right just one block north of the freeway and the cortege entrance is the second gate further north down 34th Avenue. Terminal 2 (Humphrey Terminal) of the Minneapolis–St. Paul National Airport is on adjacent property just to the west of the cemetery. As of mid-2017, more than 225,000 people are interred at Fort Snelling, and the cemetery maintains more than 172,000 gravesites.

A view just inside the main entrance of Fort Snelling National Cemetery

The Fort Snelling location was first established as a military outpost in 1805 at the confluence of the Minnesota and Mississippi rivers. It wasn't until 1820 that a permanent post named Fort St. Anthony was constructed under the supervision of Colonel Josiah Snelling. General Winfield Scott was so enamored by Snelling's leadership and the conditions there on a visit in 1824 that he recommended that the installation be renamed Fort Snelling.

Its original purpose was to keep the peace on the frontier. In 1855, as the troops kept moving west to follow the frontier, soldiers were withdrawn from Fort Snelling. During the Civil War, the fort was reopened and functioned as both an assembly ground and training camp for Minnesota volunteers. It continued to be a training ground for the U.S. Army well into the 20th century. In 1947, the Fort Snelling Military Reservation was deactivated as a post, although even today it functions as the headquarters for the 88th Army Reserve Command.

The Fort Snelling Cemetery was created in 1870 to serve as the burial ground for the soldiers who died while stationed at the post. Following WWI, as new legislation expanded the eligibility requirements for burial in a national cemetery, the citizens of Minneapolis–St. Paul organized a petition to designate a national cemetery in the area. In 1937, Congress responded with legislation that authorized a portion of land at Fort Snelling Military Reservation be designated for such a purpose.

Officially, Fort Snelling National Cemetery was established on July 4, 1939, and the first burial was on July 6. The original size of the newly–created cemetery was 223 acres. The interment was for Captain George H. Mallon, whose acts of heroism at Meuse-Argonne in France during WWI led to him being honored with the Congressional Medal of Honor.

A gravesite at Fort Snelling, one of more than 172,000. A total of 225,000 people are buried at Fort Snelling.

Following the dedication of the new cemetery, arrangements were made for the exhumation of the remains of those buried at the older post cemetery and the re-interment of the 680 soldiers who served 1820–1939 to be buried at the newly created site. The oldest grave at the old cemetery dates to 1828. The original interment sites were located just a few miles away from the present cemetery and on the Minnesota

River. Therefore, many of the graves in the original sections of the cemetery have veterans who served in the Civil War, the Spanish-American War, and World War I. The 1930s were a boom era for the construction of national cemeteries in America as the Works Progress Administration constructed many of them as part of the New Deal under Franklin D. Roosevelt. A dozen new large cemeteries were conceived between the two world wars to serve the large veteran populations in major cities across the nation.

In May of 1960, the Fort Snelling Air Force Station transferred 146 acres of land to the national cemetery. One more land transfer of 177 acres followed in 1961, bringing the cemetery to its present size. As of 2017, there are 81 memorials, most of them commemorating soldiers or the contributions of various units or branches of service of 20th-century wars. The cemetery contains a memorial pathway that is lined with veterans' memorials from various organizations.

More than 5,300 burials are conducted each year at Fort Snelling, and 2017 is on pace for the most burials in a calendar year. Currently, about 68% of the burials are cremations. The cemetery serves more than 1.4 million veterans in Minnesota, western Wisconsin, Iowa, and North and South Dakota. In 2016, the cemetery was added to the National Register of Historic Places. At current interment rates, there is space for the deceased until at least 2060 at the present site.

Visiting the Cemetery

The cemetery is open daily to the public. Gates 2 and 3 are open Monday through Friday from 8:00 a.m. to 4:15 p.m. and are closed Saturday, Sunday, and on federal holidays. The cemetery is never closed more than two days in a row for interments. Thus, if a federal holiday is on a Monday, the cemetery is open on Saturday.

Specific gravesites can be found using the automated

A view of Fort Snelling looking west, adjacent to the airport.

gravesite locator kiosk in the Public Information Center (building 1002), which is located adjacent to the main flagpole circle just inside the entrance. A nationwide gravesite locator for national cemeteries is also available at *http://www.cem.va.gov.*

Restrooms are located in the Public Information Center. Additional restrooms are located in the building adjacent to Gate 3 (open after hours and on weekends).

Visitors attending committal services gather at the designated assembly area (cortege area Gate 2) and are escorted to the proper committal shelter area by a cemetery representative. Roadway parking is available throughout the cemetery and near the committal shelter during services. Special observances and ceremonies are held in the open area at the intersection of Peck Avenue and Mallon Road (see map on page 56).

Veterans Affairs regulations 38 CFR 1.218 prohibits carrying firearms (either openly or concealed), explosives, or other dangerous or deadly weapons while on VA property. Possession of firearms on any property under the charge and control of the VA is prohibited. Offenders may be subject to a fine, removal from the premises, or arrest.

A Memorial Day ceremony is held annually at 10 a.m. on the last Monday in May, and the Memorial Rifle Squad is actively involved in its planning and execution through the Fort Snelling National Cemetery Volunteer Committee. Formed in 1946, the committee was created for the purpose of obtaining funds for projects and special needs not in the federal program. The committee is the primary planning group and sponsor for the Memorial Day ceremonies. The flagpoles used on special holidays to line the "Avenue of Flags" are supplied by the committee. While volunteers represent various veterans' organizations, the majority of them are members of the rifle squad. For specific information regarding the ceremony, call the cemetery office at (612) 726-1127 or check the website cited earlier.

While visitors are welcomed to Fort Snelling National Cemetery, they are to be reminded of its solemn purpose and

On Memorial Day, a young boy watches the start of the parade.

Winter at Fort Snelling National Cemetery

are to act in a dignified manner while on the cemetery grounds. For this reason, public gatherings of a partisan nature are not permitted. In addition, sports or recreational activities are not permitted, including bicycle riding, jogging, picnicking, roller-blading, walking pets, fishing, or hunting. Police and fire protection for the cemetery is provided by multiple organizations, including the Veterans Affairs Police Department, the Hennepin County Sheriff's Office, and the Metropolitan Airport Authority.

Cemetery floral policies are posted on the floral storage receptacles located throughout the cemetery. Fresh-cut flowers are welcomed throughout the year, and flower containers for gravesite displays are provided as a courtesy to visitors. Once the flowers become unsightly, they are removed; they can also be removed to allow for routine mowing or other maintenance.

Limited floral arrangements accompanying the casket or urn at the time of burial can be placed on the completed grave. Artificial flowers and potted plants are allowed for graves for a period of 10 days before and 10 days after Easter Sunday and Memorial Day. Seasonal holiday adornments such as

Christmas wreaths, potted poinsettias and other seasonal items may be placed on graves from December 1 through January 20.

To maintain the dignity of the cemetery, permanent plants, statues, balloons, pinwheels, vigil lights, breakable objects, and similar items are not permitted on the graves. The Department of Veteran Affairs does not permit adornments that are considered offensive, inconsistent with the dignity of the cemetery, or considered hazardous to cemetery personnel. For example, items incorporating wires may become entangled in mowers or other equipment and cause injury.

ADMINISTRATION

Fort Snelling National Cemetery is administered by the National Cemetery Administration within the auspices of the Department of Veteran Affairs, and its headquarters are located in the administration building near the main entrance. The current executive director is Ame Callahan, who started in her post on June 26, 2017. This is a newly created position as the five busiest cemeteries (Fort Snelling is fourth) in the system were given the authority to hire an executive director.

Callahan, in her fourth year with the NCA, had a 24-year career in the Air Force and finished her active duty as a Chief Master Sergeant. Raised in a foster home in Thailand, she was adopted at age 14 by her father, a Vietnam veteran. She lived in Wisconsin and Illinois before joining the service in 1977.

Nearly all of my dealings with the top management at Fort Snelling National Cemetery, however, were with then-director and now deputy director John G. Knapp, who has been at Fort Snelling since August of 2014. A died-in-the-wool Marine, he can be contacted by phone at (612) 467-4619 or e-mail at *john.knapp@va.gov*. The administration office is open Monday through Friday from 8 a.m. to 4:15 p.m. and is closed on designated holidays.

On a visit one wintry morning, I find Knapp to be a dynamic

and engaging personality and someone who relishes his position. An imposing physical figure who looks like he could still
manage basic training in San Diego with ease, Knapp is de-
lighted to represent his country in his current position. It becomes clear quickly that Knapp is a leader and a big proponent
of the Memorial Rifle Squad's role at Fort Snelling.

Dressed in a coat and tie in an office adorned with the red,
white, and blue, the square-jawed 54-year-old with the crew-
cut says, "I am proud to be working for our veterans and to be
able to honor them by having the best possible cemetery. We
want to provide a dignified final farewell to our military personnel, and as George Weiss always says, 'It's our mission and
it's what we do,' and we know that the Memorial Rifle Squad
has a special role in our operation."

Knapp grew up in suburban Pittsburgh and received his
degree in education (secondary social studies) from Edinboro
University in Edinboro, Pennsylvania. He also holds an M.B.A.
in Aviation Administration from Embry-Riddle Aeronautical
University and is currently using his post-911 G.I. Bill toward
completion of a master's in international relations from Oklahoma University.

John remains a die-hard Steelers fan, but the Eagan resident is now a Vikings season ticket holder, too. He served in
the Marine Corps 1985–97 on active duty and again 2001–03.
John also had two stints in the Reserve (1997–2001 and 2003–
11). Knapp finished flight school and became a Harrier pilot
in 1991 and reached the rank of Lt. Colonel. From 2006–14,
Knapp worked as a civilian war planner for the Deputy Chief
of War Plans at Camp Smith in Honolulu, Hawaii, writing
strategy for possible war plans in the Pacific. An opportunity arose at Fort Snelling, and Knapp arrived in Minnesota to
work at one of the best cemeteries in the nation.

Asked about his feelings about the Memorial Rifle Squad,
he flashes a wide smile and says, "We work hand-in-glove, and

I have great respect for what they do. While they are officially a non-military group, they are considered Veterans Affairs volunteers, and we give them space, an office, and the requisite communication to provide respectful funerals for our deceased veterans and their families. They are a tremendous group, and they are the model for the rest of the nation. They are a critical component to what we do out here."

"The only thing we buy for the rifle squad is the ammunition," remarks Knapp, who is highly respected by members of the rifle squad. "They provide everything else themselves, and we love working with them. In fact, when they purchased their new van a few years ago, they bought it themselves and then donated it to the U.S. government, and it has official government plates on it."

The cemetery has 50 full-time-equivalent workers, and currently 82 percent of them are veterans. Thus, there is a built-in camaraderie among the staff and a clear understanding of the importance of the job. The cemetery also employs 8 to 12 temporary laborers in the summer to meet the increased demands of that season.

"Our staff quietly goes about their business serving the nation in their own capacity," adds Knapp. "They have a level of dedication that is unmatched in the private sector. You give them a mission and the work gets done; they are very dependable. Whether they are in the office or out in the acreage, our people know that they play a significant role in what we do out here."

Queried about the rules regarding eligibility for interment, Knapp says, "Congress determines the rules regarding who can be buried at a federal cemetery, so we don't have any control over that." Recently, the Department of Veterans Affairs promulgated a positive new change regarding eligibility. "You used to have to wait until after someone died to determine eligibility for burial at a federal cemetery," he states. "Now, if there is any question about eligibility, it can be determined while they are still living. Once a document is filed regarding an application to be buried, the VA does the research to see if you qualify. This pre-need application, started in 2016, has become a very popular program, and it makes it so much easier on the family once the death occurs."

To ensure proper support to the large veteran population serviced by the Fort Snelling National Cemetery, several contracts have been established and impact the local economy. They include services for broadleaf weed control, trash and garbage collection, wildlife management, work therapy, apple seed and emerald ash borer treatment, on-site headstone/marker inscription, grave liner installation, and mowing/trimming/edging/sod.

Knapp states, "We have a great working relationship with these contractors, and we enjoy a unique partnership with the community. We are proud to work with them to maintain one of the finest cemeteries in our system."

John Knapp knows that the Memorial Rifle Squad holds a special niche in the cemetery's legacy. "What the Memorial Rifle Squad does is so critical to what we do here," says an emphatic Knapp. "George Weiss and his squads have created something so special that truly makes the funerals out here so memorable and touching. Without their honor ceremony, we would just be mediocre."

"I have enjoyed every minute of my time here at Fort Snelling," continues Knapp. "I love what I have been doing, just taking care of veterans and their families. It is really quite simple—for 15 minutes, we try to stop the world for the family of the deceased. We try to give them, and their departed loved one who served, the honor, dignity, and respect they so richly deserve. We strive to show them how important their service was to the nation and that we will also take good care of them perpetually. I am so proud of the Memorial Rifle Squad and what they orchestrate for us."

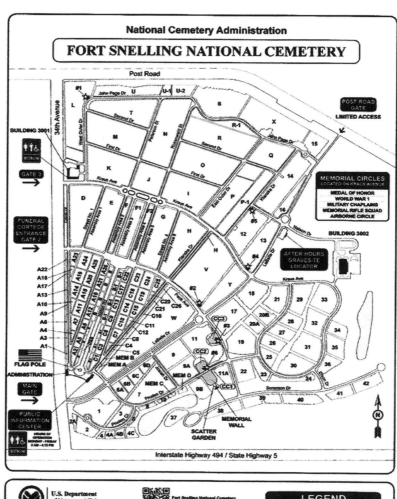

Chapter 5

Medal of Honor Recipients

While 56 Minnesotans have earned the Congressional Medal of Honor for their bravery and heroism representing the United States military, only eight of them are interred (and one memorialized) at Fort Snelling National Cemetery. Biographies of these individuals appear below.

RICHARD EUGENE FLEMING

Captain Richard E. Fleming (November 12, 1917–June 5, 1942) was a United States Marine who received the Medal of Honor for his heroism in WWII during the battle of Midway. Fleming piloted a Vought SB2U dive bomber in an attack on the Japanese cruiser *Mikuma*.

Fleming was born in St. Paul and attended St. Thomas Military Academy, where he graduated at the top of his class in 1935. He then received his B.A. from the University of Minnesota in 1939. After enlisting in the Marine Corps Reserves, he finished at the top of his flight training class at the Naval Air Station in Pensacola, Florida. On June 4, 1942, he took command of his bombing squadron after his commander was shot down. Leaving his formation, he dove to a low altitude to score a hit on a Japanese aircraft carrier, exposing himself to heavy enemy fire. His plane was hit by 179 bullets, but he suffered just two minor injuries. He arrived back at base despite hazardous weather and total darkness.

After less than four hours of sleep, Captain Fleming led his squadron on a mass dive-bombing assault on the *Mikuma* the next day. His plane dove low and was hit by anti-aircraft fire. The plane crashed into the sea and he perished. For "extraordinary heroism and conspicuous gallantry above and beyond the call of duty," the Captain was posthumously awarded the nation's highest military decoration when President Franklin Roosevelt presented the Medal of Honor to Fleming's mother on Nov. 24, 1942.

The USS *Fleming*, commissioned on Sept. 18, 1943, was named in his honor, and a memorial to him is placed within Fort Snelling. Captain Fleming's name is listed on the Tablets of the Missing at the Punchbowl Federal Cemetery in Honolulu, Hawaii. Fleming is also memorialized each year at his

The grave of Richard E. Fleming, one of the eight Medal of Honor awardees buried at Fort Snelling. Fleming, a Marine pilot, died during the Battle of Midway in WWII.

alma mater, St. Thomas Academy in Mendota Heights, during the Cadet Colonel promotion ceremony. Richard E. Fleming Field is also the name for the South St. Paul Municipal Airport.

RICHARD E. KRAUS

Private First-Class Richard Edward Kraus (November 24, 1925–October 3, 1944) was a United States Marine killed in action during the WWII campaign on Peleliu Island on Oct. 3, 1944. Kraus had been overseas only three months at the time of the Peleliu battle, which was his first campaign. On the occasion of his heroism and death, the 18-year-old was serving as an amphibious tractor driver.

Kraus and three others in his battalion accepted a volunteer mission to evacuate a wounded Marine from the front lines. Moving forward, the group was met by an intense barrage of grenade fire and was forced to take cover. While returning to the rear, the stretcher party observed two men approaching, believing they were Marines. However, they proved to be Japanese soldiers and one of them responded by throwing a grenade into their midst. Kraus, without hesitation, hurled himself on top of the grenade. His prompt action and personal valor in the face of certain death saved the lives of his three comrades.

The Edison graduate had been inducted into the Marine Corps on his 18th birthday. Born in Chicago, he moved to Minneapolis as a seven-year-old. The United States Navy destroyer USS *Richard E. Kraus* was named in his honor and the Assault Amphibian Schools Battalion at Camp Pendleton, California, was also named and dedicated in his memory. He was initially buried in the U.S. Armed Forces Cemetery on Peleliu Island. In 1948, his remains were reinterred at Fort Snelling at his parents' request.

JAMES D. LABELLE

Private First-Class James Dennis LaBelle (November 25, 1925–March 8, 1945) was a U.S. Marine who was killed in action on Iwo Jima on March 8, 1945. LaBelle sacrificed his life when he launched himself onto a hostile grenade hoisted into his foxhole. The Private from the Twin Cities had dug a foxhole with two other Marines and was grimly aware of the persistent efforts by the enemy to blast through their lines with hand grenades.

The Medal of Honor citation stated, in part, "Without hesitation, he relinquished his own chance of survival that his fellow Marines might carry on the relentless fight against a fanatical enemy and his dauntless courage, cool decision and variant spirit of self-sacrifice in the face of certain death reflect the highest credit upon Private LaBelle."

LaBelle was a member of the 27th Marine Regiment and was trained in the intensive combat training course at Camp Pendleton before embarking for overseas. He reached the lava shores of Iwo Jima on February 19, 1945, and fought continuously for nearly three weeks before his untimely death.

Born in Columbia Heights, James enjoyed raising homing pigeons. In high school, he starred on the baseball, basketball, and boxing teams. LaBelle also liked to work with wood and metals and worked as an apprentice welder before enlisting in the Marines Reserves at age 17 in 1943 with his mother's permission.

His mother was presented the Medal of Honor by the Director of the Marine Corps in ceremonies conducted on July 21, 1946, in Minneapolis. LaBelle's remains were returned to the U.S. in 1948 and were reinterred at Fort Snelling.

GEORGE H. MALLON

Captain George H. Mallon (June 15, 1877–August 2, 1934) was an officer in the United States Army who received the Medal of Honor for his actions during WWI. A Kansas native, Mallon was in the 132nd Infantry Regiment and the 33rd Infantry Division when he earned the highest military designation in a battle at Bois-de-Forges, France, on September 26, 1918.

Separated from the majority of his company, Mallon and nine other soldiers pushed forward in a fog and attacked several active machine-gun positions. They captured all of the enemy without loss of a man. The Captain then attacked a battery of howitzers, capturing the battery and its crew. When confronted with more machine-gun fire, he later sent the other men to the flanks while he rushed forward directly in the face of enemy fire and silenced the guns, being the first of his party to reach the nest. Captain Mallon's gallantry and determination resulted in the capture of 100 prisoners, 11 machine guns, four 155-millimeter howitzers, and one anti-aircraft gun.

Mallon was also given the Legion of Honor and the Croix de Guerre from France. George was honorably discharged in June of 1919 and died on August 2, 1934, at the age of 57 in St. Cloud.

OSCAR F. NELSON

Oscar Frederick Nelson (November 5, 1881–September 26, 1951) was awarded a rare peacetime Medal of Honor for his life-saving efforts as a Machinist's Mate First Class in the U.S. Navy aboard the USS *Bennington* on July 21, 1905. His citation was granted on January 6, 1906.

Docked off Point Loma in San Diego Bay, two boilers on the gunboat exploded and instantly killed many seamen. Dozens of others were thrown overboard, and the ship began taking on water. Nelson rescued many of his shipmates before the ship sank. The Navy man saved more than a half-dozen of his compatriots gulping hot steam as they screamed in pain. He made several trips to the lower decks, making sure all his fellow shipmates (dead or alive) were out. The disaster killed 66 Navy personnel and maimed 49 others. Of the 30 men working below deck, Nelson was the lone survivor. Over half of the crew was killed or wounded.

Born in Minneapolis 1881, the son of Dutch immigrants joined the Navy in 1899. Nelson was discharged in 1911 and later served for 24 years with the U.S. Army Corps of Engineers in Duluth. His Congressional Medal of Honor is on display at the Canal Park Marine Museum there as part of its Peacetime Collection. Oscar died at the age of 70 on September 26, 1951. He and his wife, Anna, who outlived him by 30 years, are interred together at Fort Snelling.

ARLO L. OLSON

Captain Arlo L. Olson (April 20, 1918–October 28, 1943) was a member of the United States Army and was killed in action on

October 28, 1943, at Monte San Nicola, Italy, during a WWII battle. For weeks in the fall of 1943, Olson repeatedly led his men in attacks against German forces, personally capturing several enemy positions until he was mortally wounded during a reconnaissance patrol.

Age 25 at his death, Olson was posthumously awarded the Medal of Honor ten months later on August 31, 1944. He was an Eagle Scout and one of nine Eagle Scouts who were awarded the Medal of Honor.

Born in Iowa and raised in South Dakota, Olson attended South Dakota University and then was commissioned through the Army ROTC following graduation. By October of 1943, he was serving as a Captain in the 15th Infantry Regiment and the 3rd Infantry Division. He demonstrated conspicuous leadership during the push across the Volturno River in Italy.

Olson and his company spearheaded the advance of the regiment through 30 miles of mountainous terrain in enemy territory in 13 days. On numerous occasions, he exhibited great personal bravery, leading combat patrols, acting as a lead scout, and maintaining unbroken contact with the enemy. After a series of heroic charges at the enemy, Captain Olson led his group toward the summit of Monte San Nicola.

Despite furious automatic and small-arms fire, Olson waved his company into a skirmish line and ultimately drove the enemy away. While doing reconnaissance to establish defensive positions, Olson was fatally wounded. Ignoring severe pain, the intrepid officer completed his task by supervising the location of his men—all the while refusing medical aid until all his men had been cared for. He died as he was being carried down the mountain.

Robert J. Pruden

Staff Sergeant Robert Joseph Pruden (September 9, 1949–November 29, 1969) was a member of the United States Army and received the Medal of Honor for his distinguished actions in Quang Ngai Province, Republic of Vietnam, on November 29, 1969. Pruden, age 20, was killed in a firefight with enemy forces and received his award posthumously after serving with the 75th Ranger Infantry Regiment (Airborne).

The young Minnesotan was serving as a reconnaissance team leader during an ambush mission. The six-man team was dropped by helicopter into enemy-controlled territory to obtain information concerning enemy movements. Quickly, the team was the object of fierce gunfire. With full knowledge of the extreme danger, Pruden left his concealed position and, firing as he ran, advanced toward the enemy to draw the hostile fire. He was seriously wounded twice but continued until he fell for the third time, directly in front of the enemy position. His actions resulted in several enemy casualties and the withdrawal of their force. Although grievously injured, he directed his men into defensive positions and called for evacuation helicopters.

DONALD RUDOLPH, SR.

Second Lieutenant Donald Eugene Rudolph (February 21, 1921–May 25, 2006) was a member of the U.S. Army during WWII and received his country's highest honor for his heroic activities fighting in the Philippines on February 5, 1945. Just short of his 24th birthday, the South Haven, Minnesota, native was serving as a technical sergeant and acting as leader of his platoon on Luzon Island.

While giving first aid on the battlefield, he noticed that his unit was pinned down by gunfire from a ditch. He crawled to the ditch and killed three enemy soldiers concealed there. Rudolph continued to work his way across open ground to a line of pillboxes that were immobilizing his company. After silencing several machine-gunners, he ordered several riflemen to cover his advance as he proceeded to neutralize seven more pillboxes in quick succession. With complete disregard for his own safety, Rudolph later approached an enemy tank under heavy fire and negated its threat.

He was immediately promoted to Second Lieutenant after the battle. President Harry Truman presented Rudolph with his well-deserved award on August 23, 1945. Rudolph continued his Army career in the Reserves until 1963 and then worked in the Veterans Administration until his retirement in 1976. Rudolph died from complications of Alzheimer's disease in Grand Rapids, Minnesota, on May 25, 2006. On U.S. Highway 7 north from Highway 169 to Bigfork, Minnesota, in northern Minnesota, a commemorative site identifies that stretch of road as the Donald Rudolph Medal of Honor Scenic Byway.

RICHARD K. SORENSON

First Lieutenant Richard Keith Sorenson (August 28, 1924–October 9, 2004) was a United States Marine, who, as a private, received the Medal of Honor during WWII for his heroism during the landing on Kwajalein Atoll (Marshall Islands) in the Pacific on the night of February 1, 1944. After a Japanese soldier threw a grenade in the midst of his squad, Sorenson launched himself on the exploding grenade in order to save the lives of five fellow Marines.

Amazingly, although fragments ripped through his thighs, hips, right arm, and right leg, he lived through the action. Of the 27 Marines known to have thrown themselves on grenades to save others during WWII, Sorenson was one of only four who survived. After recovering from his serious wounds (six surgeries in nine months), Sorenson remained in the Corps until he was discharged in 1946 at the rank of Sergeant. He enlisted in the Reserves in 1947 and reached the rank of Master Sergeant and received a commission as an officer in 1953.

The son of a U.S. Navy veteran of WWI, Richard was born in Anoka, Minnesota, and graduated from high school in 1942. He enlisted in the Marines and landed at Namur, Kwajalein, and was wounded in action on his first night of combat.

After leaving the Marine Corps in 1955, Sorenson returned to work for the Veterans Administration until 1957. For 10 years, he worked as an insurance underwriter before returning to the VA in 1967. He remained with the VA until his retirement in 1985 as Director of Veteran Affairs for the state of Nevada and nine counties of California. Sorenson died at age 80 in Reno, Nevada, and was buried with full military honors at Fort Snelling.

Six of the Medal of Honor recipients (Kraus, LaBelle, Mallon, Olson, Nelson, and Pruden) have major thoroughfares within the cemetery named after them, but all are recognized with memorials in the cemetery. Other noteworthy individuals who have their final resting place at Fort Snelling include:

Thomas Barnett, Jr., a Bloomington native and former Jefferson High School quarterback who died on Sept, 11, 2001, aboard United Flight 93 while attempting to prevent a terrorist attack on Washington, D.C.

Halsey Hall, entertaining sportswriter and broadcaster for more than 50 years.

C. Walton Lillehei, a pioneer in heart surgery at the University of Minnesota.

Charles Lindberg, a U.S. Marine who was one of six to raise the original flag on Mt. Suribachi on Iwo Jima on Feb. 23, 1945.

John Mariucci, an Eveleth native considered the godfather of Minnesota hockey, who coached at the University of Minnesota, played and was an exexutive in the NHL, and is a member of the U.S. Hockey Hall of Fame and the Hockey Hall of Fame in Toronto.

Bruce Smith, a Faribault native and Gopher football star who won the 1941 Heisman Trophy.

Chapter 6

Tuesday Squad

Over parts of three years, I spent numerous days with each of the weekday rifle squads. There wasn't a time when I wasn't entertained or amused. There wasn't a time when I wasn't awed by the group's dedication and their resolute loyalty to their unified cause. Good humor was a constant, along with brutal honesty, and the camaraderie was contagious.

The squads are listed in the order in which they were created; first Tuesday, then Friday, Thursday, Wednesday, and finally, Monday. Tuesday was the only day of the week that funerals were conducted during the first months of the Memorial Rifle Squad. The Friday squad started on September 10, 1979; the Thursday squad began in January of 1980, the Wednesday squad started in the fall of 1980, and the Monday contingent began in January of 1981.

My first official visit to observe one of the volunteer squads came early in 2015. That first visit was with the Tuesday squad, the first day of the week established by the rifle squad. It was a typical cold mid-January day but with a beautiful cobalt sky. The temperature was 10 degrees below zero and the wind-chill factor was -25. The cemetery was adorned with early-morning shadows, and I stopped to take a few pictures of the gravestones and the perfect geometric lines, with many of the graves still bedecked with thousands of Christmas wreaths.

The Tuesday squad gathers at the main flagpole near the administration buildings in August 2017.

The Memorial Rifle Squad's headquarters are attached to the maintenance facility for the cemetery that is located at the eastern end of the cemetery, not far from the edge of Minneapolis–St. Paul airport and a couple football-field lengths from I-494. The room was added on to the maintenance building in April of 2009 but is surprisingly small. When I arrived at the squad room at 8:45 a.m., then squad leader Archie W. Hazzard was in the midst of his administrative duties. Archie, as is his custom, was at his post by 7:00 a.m. to make sure all arrangements were set for the day. The former Marine quickly stood and told his group the reason for my arrival and then jokingly asked if they were in favor of me being there. Everybody laughed. It was obvious this is a place where people feel at home.

Hazzard, a genial fellow who has the ability to make everyone around him feel comfortable, has been on the squad for 15 years and served as the overall Commander in 2010. Archie grew up on the east side of St. Paul and played hockey with

Herb Brooks at St. Paul Johnson, though the furthest he got was as a B-squad goalie. After graduating in 1953, Hazzard enlisted right away in the Marine Corps and served 1953–56. He was in the 1st Marine Division and was a Sergeant in the infantry. Most of his time was spent serving at Camp Pendleton in California after spending a year in Korea, though the armistice was signed just before his induction. He has lived in Lakeland for over 30 years. He laid linoleum and other hard surface flooring for decades, mostly for Jennings D. McClellan, his father-in-law. After retirement in 1999, he joined the Tuesday squad in 2000.

"My dad died in 1982, and I said I was going to serve on the rifle squad someday," states Hazzard. "I knew a guy from Tuesday, so I went out and visited and was able to join up. Later, I took over as squad leader from Hugh Heckel, who helped build the Tuesday group. He and many others did a great job establishing this outfit."

Unfortunately, Archie had to resign from his service with the Tuesday squad later in 2015 to care for his wife, Jackie. However, that did not prevent him from getting into uniform once again on July 11, 2017. He was present for the funeral of Harold Stener, who had served on Tuesdays 1995–2012. Archie was allowed to be the flag presenter that solemn day as the Tuesday squad buried one of their own.

"I was able to present the flag to Harold's son on that day, and it meant a lot to be able to do that," says Hazzard. "The family was so impressed with what I had to say that they later called me at home to thank me. It shows that people really appreciate what we do. It's an honor to do it and especially meaningful when it's one of our guys."

While the funeral services don't officially begin until 10:00 a.m. each day, it is readily apparent that these guys got here early by evidence of the banter and gentle ease with which they deal with each other. About 10 fellows are already present for the day and dressed in appropriate clothing for the harsh elements. One foursome plays cards near the back of the room, while the others commiserate about the health of one of their team members. Archie bemoans the recent terrible play of the local NHL team, the Wild, to St. Paul fire captain Rich Zech, a St. Bernard's alumnus who has been on the squad for nine years. Zech had stopped at the V.A. hospital cafeteria nearby to pick up soup for that day's lunch.

As I begin to arrange my journalistic tools (miniature tape recorder, notebook, et al.), the incessant teasing and needling becomes widespread. It's good-natured, but funny and disarming at the same time. One gentleman inquires about whether two other members will show up on this cold morn and another shouts out, "They're wimps." Everybody cackled.

Archie Hazzard is assigning the members to their specific tasks for the day and announces that it will be a fairly light day for funerals, with only seven on the docket. Sandy Kleinke and Ted Zwart, both in their first months with the rifle squad, walk by, and another volunteer tells me that the pair drive from Elysian to do their once-a-week duty. I know my Minnesota geography and know it is not far from Mankato. Sandy tells me it is 72 miles one-way to get to Fort Snelling when they carpool for their duty.

With 45 minutes to go before the first funeral, there is conversation about the terrorist shootings in Paris the previous week amidst zingers regarding belonging to the wrong military service and the snow-birds who aren't with them. The Marines and Army guys seem to have the most fun berating each other. At the same time, there is genuine concern for other members of the Tuesday squad as Archie and assistant squad leader Dan Fisher speak about a gentleman who is about to have surgery and a few others who are still recovering from various ailments. Cards will be sent out from the well-wishers.

Roman Rowan, a gregarious Navy veteran, seats himself

Roman Rowan plays "Taps" in frigid conditions.

next to me and begins a stirring conversation. He has been with the rifle squad for eight years. Roman was in the high school band at Richfield High and played the trumpet, a precursor to serving as the bugler for the Tuesday squad. A software consultant before retirement, he also serves with the Police Reserves in Plymouth, where he now resides. Now 76 years old, Roman belongs to VFW Post 5903 in Hamel and Legion Post 394 in the same city. Rowan served four years as a 2nd Class Petty Officer, including two years in the Philippines.

It's obvious he is an engaging and well-rounded individual and he answers many of the basic questions I have about the regimen of the typical funeral and the duties of specific jobs. I query him about the difficulty of bugling on such bitterly-cold days. Roman says, "I stay in the van as long as I can and I put my mouth-piece in my glove until I am signaled to begin playing 'Taps.'" He ends up doing a marvelous job all day.

Soon, he tells me that he has this wonderful story about

serving on the rifle squad. He is not sure who he heard it from but he thinks it is one that might befit the book. It came well before he joined the organization. Apparently, there was a father and a young son attending a service at Fort Snelling. With the Memorial Rifle Squad at their appointed positions, the father points to them and tells the son, "See those guys standing at attention, those are the fellows who saved our country." Immediately, the son retorts, "You mean, those old guys"? Roman roars and so do I. Everybody wonders what we are laughing about. So, the story is retold, amid more laughter and nodding.

Roman finds out that I am a big baseball fan and that I wrote a book on the Minnesota Twins. He pulls out what looks like a baseball card. It is a photo of him and his bride, Connie, on their wedding day at Lee County Stadium in Ft. Myers, Florida. The date February 8, 1992, is stamped on the card, and Roman is in a Twins' uniform with the number 55, while his gorgeous beloved is in a traditional white wedding dress. Among the attendees listed on the back besides their family members are some of my heroes from the 1960s—Tony Oliva, Rich Rollins, Early Battey, and Jim "Mudcat" Grant.

As 10:00 a.m. approaches, the volunteers make sure they are ready for the day. There is some muttering about the weather, but I can sense that the mood is about to change. While there is still some bantering, it gets a bit quieter as the 14-man contingent this day saunters out into the stark winter sun. They walk a short distance to get in a Ford van that can seat up to 26 people. It is a new, just purchased in the fall of 2014 for about $86,000, and it is paid for by the squad itself. I ask Archie Hazzard how they can afford it. As he climbs into the van, he states, "We get a lot of donations." The other fellows concur and one says, "I guess the families that come here to bury their loved ones appreciate what we are doing."

The assistant squad leader, Daniel J. Fisher, served as the overall Commander of the rifle squad in 2013. He grew up in

Dan Fisher, squad leader, leads a meeting prior to the day's services.

the Frogtown area of St. Paul and graduated from St. Agnes High School in 1965. A sergeant in the Marines 1966–68, Dan served 13 months in Vietnam in the infantry and earned a Purple Heart. Following his service, the Oakdale resident spent 35 years at 3M as a research specialist and is an active member of VFW Post 1350 in North St. Paul.

Fisher recalls, "I remember coming out to Fort Snelling in 1976 for the funeral of a good buddy of mine who was my squad leader in Vietnam; he had survived the war but died at age 29 while playing hockey. There were no military honors for him. Long after the honor guard was established, I was present for the dedication of a monument for the 5th Marine Division, which was my outfit. In 2004, I was at a breakfast at work when I saw a guy wearing a rifle squad jacket and I asked him about the group. It was Archie Hazzard and he told me to come and observe the Tuesday squad. So, I did and I have been with them ever since." In 2015, Hazard had to become inactive in order to take care of his wife, and Fisher stepped in seamlessly as the squad leader.

"Each of the squads has its own culture and chemistry," states the confident yet cordial Fisher. "However, we all try to do things in a uniform fashion when we conduct our services for the deceased veteran." It is obvious that Fisher relishes his role and that his leadership, wisdom, and common sense are appreciated by his men. He is also proud that his son was a Marine and that his grandson, recently graduated from North St. Paul High, was to be inducted into the Marine Corps in late July of 2017.

Richard R. Zech is one of the younger members of the rifle squad. At age 63, he has served for 11 years with the Tuesday squad. Virtually all of the other volunteers are retired. Zech is still working full-time as a St. Paul fire captain, the top officer for Ladder 18, not far from his boyhood home on Rice Street. Because he works 24-hour shifts in his job with the capital city, the only day he can volunteer at the cemetery is Tuesday.

After graduating from St. Bernard's High, Zech enlisted in the Navy and served 1973–77 on the USS *Caloosahatchee* as an electrician's mate. The ship was based in Norfolk, Virginia, but he spent most of his seaside time in the North Atlantic. A sports enthusiast, he still looks fit enough to breeze through basic training. He's a member of Legion Post 533 on the east side of St. Paul, and like many others on the squad, he rotates responsibilities on the days he serves.

"When I first started with the rifle squad, the funerals were a little tough to deal with and were pretty emotional for me," says Zech. "I was in awe of the sacrifice and valor of many of the guys on the squad, especially the WWII vets who had seen a lot of heavy action in either the Pacific or the European Theater. Now, those guys were really heroes."

Zech first witnessed the rifle squad's presence when he attended his own father's funeral on December 23, 2002. He states, "The ceremony for Dad, who was in the 103rd infantry, was just beautiful. It was a very cold Friday, I remember, but I felt the presence of the honor guard and knew I wanted to do this someday. A few years later, I came out to the main building and explained that I wanted to join but I was still working. It worked out that I could serve on Tuesdays, and it's just been a great experience."

Dennis W. Lande, who assisted both Hazzard and Fisher for several years as assistant squad leader, is a courteous fellow who is both knowledgeable and helpful to a novice inquiring about rifle squad operations. A Winona High grad of 1966, Lande attended Winona State until enlisting in the Marine Corps early in 1968. After training at Camp Pendleton and San Diego in California, Lande was attached to an air wing working in air traffic control (MATCU). The Corporal spent three years on active duty, most of it in Okinawa, and most enjoyed spending a year teaching electronics.

After 32 years as an elementary and middle school science teacher and elementary principal for South Washington County schools, Lande saddled up with the rifle squad in 2006. Less than a week after retiring, Dennis was working the daily funerals. "I was aware of the rifle squads after seeing it online years before, and I knew I wanted to do something," said Lande. "I talked to Ted Nemzek about it and found out there was an opening on Tuesday. I came out to observe, and my squad leader, Hugh Heckel, had me start right away."

Possessing a perfectly dignified manner, the 69-year-old Lande serves as a presenter to the families. He states, "I really enjoy serving the veteran's family, and it makes the service very real. It's so nice to be a comfort to them during their time of need. I had no dangerous duty while on active duty so I think I owe it to the other vets who saw combat to still serve, and that's why I do this. Also, many of these guys have become very good friends—Dan Fisher, Gerry Ballot, and Kent Petrie."

Lande, whose father served in the Army Air Corps, relays an amazing story about one of his early funeral experiences.

"I was presenting for a Native American veteran, and the family was just finishing the drum ceremony," he remarks. "After presenting the flag, I was walking away from the committal area and all of a sudden, I witnessed a bald eagle circling above the shelter. Wow! Not only is it our country's symbol but it is sacred in their culture, of course. It was meant to be."

Lande now works part-time as a supervisor of student teachers as an adjunct professor for Winona State University. A resident of Blaine for 12 years, he is now in his 12th year at that position and is active with Legion Post 566 in Lino Lakes.

Gerald D. Holmer is a diminutive former Army veteran who served two years in the mid-1950s as a corporal, mostly at Fort Carson, Colorado. He smiles and says, "If you remember 'M.A.S.H.', I was like Radar. I took typing in high school so I managed the office and was responsible for troop information and just about anything, even though I started out as a medic." A gentle soul, Gerald joined the Tuesday group in 2000 and usually carries the American flag and he says it's all due to seniority. Holmer, now 84, was a rifleman for many years.

Holmer was raised in northeast Minneapolis and attended Edison before transferring to Minnehaha Academy. Following his active duty, he worked in the insurance industry, mainly with injury claims for the final 25 years. A Fridley resident for over 40 years, he is a member of Legion Post 303 in that northern suburb.

"After I retired in 1999, it took me a couple months to get thoroughly bored," states Holmer. "I happened to find out that the rifle squad needed guys, especially on Tuesday, and it worked out. When you are a rifleman or carry the flags, you don't get to interact with the people who attend the funeral very often. But one time, a guy came up as I was getting back on the bus and he had two little kids with him, and he asked if they could get the shell casings from the rifle volleys."

The color guard and rifle squad stand at attention as the remains of a veteran are brought to the catafalque.

"Apparently, the deceased was the grandfather of the two little boys," continues Gerald. "We told them that, of course, it was okay. They started stuffing their pockets with the shells, and the father was in tears as he told me that his dad had landed with the troops at Normandy on the first day of D-Day. That was a pretty special moment and makes me even more aware of how special the ceremony can be to the loved ones."

James F. McGee grew up in St. Paul and graduated from Wilson High. Jim spent 31 years as a pressman for the Waldorf Corporation in St. Paul. After retirement, McGee joined the rifle squad in 2006. The gray-bearded White Bear Lake resident served in the U.S. Navy 1959–63, mostly on a tugboat on the Columbia River, and was based out of Astoria, Oregon. From 1983–1995, Jim was a part of a Reserve unit involved with amphibious construction in the state of Virginia. Now 75 years old, he belongs to Legion Post 168 in White Bear Lake.

An uncle of McGee, a highly awarded soldier who fought at Iwo Jima, Guadalcanal, and Peleliu, died and was buried in Sioux Falls, South Dakota, about 20 years ago. There were no military honors. McGee says, "I was at the burial and having no honor guard there really bothered me."

"I heard through the grapevine that the Tuesday squad was looking for a bugler," adds the mild-mannered McGee. "Aboard the *Helena* I had been a bugler, but that was many years ago. I called the cemetery office and left my number, and Hugh Heckel, the squad leader at that time, called me and invited me out for a visit. I played for him and the next week, I was playing with Clarence Kraemer, and we played together for 11 years. I really had to work to get better, though, and I practiced two hours each day and seven days a week for 11 years so I could represent myself properly."

A bout with Bell's palsy and Parkinson's disease, however, has now relegated Jim to flag duty. He quietly says, "I'm lucky to be still out here, and I'm lucky that they still want me out here." McGee struggles to walk to the bus for the day's funerals—true inspiration and dedication, indeed.

Ricky L. Youngmark is a forthright individual with a can-do spirit. The 63-year-old grew up in Faribault and graduated from St. James High School. H was an aircraft mechanic in the Air Force and served for 11 years. Ricky enjoyed working on F-111 jets and had several stops—Grand Forks, North Dakota; Panama City, Florida; Great Falls, Montana; and Mountain View, Idaho; in addition to several locations in Europe.

Prior to his joining the military with the "buddy" system in 1972, Youngmark had attended college at Winona State, and while there he was in the Army Reserves for two years in Wabasha. After his discharge, Ricky worked as an aircraft mechanic for American Airlines (based in Tulsa, Oklahoma) for 26 years and retired in 2010. He had transferred to Minneapolis in 2000.

These days, Youngmark drives from his home in Cannon Falls, where he has resided for 17 years. He is a member of Legion Post 84 in Northfield. He has trained in each role on the squad yet loves the opportunity to be a rifleman. Ricky was added to the Tuesday grouping in 2011, and his comportment clearly indicates that he relishes everything about serving with his squad.

"I've met a lot of new people on this squad and now they are some of my best friends," says Youngmark. "It's important that we honor our veterans, but we also do a lot of stuff together outside the cemetery, too, and that is also important to our brotherhood. My wife had worked for the Minneapolis Veterans Home in administration, and she was well aware of the rifle squads and informed me all about them."

Another fellow who lived in Cannon Falls and was on the Tuesday squad was the beloved former Marine, Bernie Melter, who served for 15 years and died in 2015. "Bernie's funeral was on a Tuesday and it was very special," adds Ricky. "We had a fly-over, and then we had a unique thing where we have the flag and go forward 10 feet and then have the rifleman go up and present arms."

Fermin L. (Lee) Aragon grew up living in several locations in the American Southwest as his family looked for employment as migrant workers. Not a full-fledged member of the squad at the time of my visit, he was on his third observation visit to the Tuesday squad. Aragon served in the Army 1965–69, including a year in Vietnam as a Sergeant. Now 72, he lives in Tonka Bay after a long career as an entrepreneur, mostly as a business consultant. Lee owned his own business for the entirety of his career and now belongs to Legion Post 580 in Chanhassen, where he has joined their honor guard.

"I read an article in the *Star Tribune* about the rifle squad," says the reserved Aragon. "After seeing that, I said that's something I would really enjoy. I was only on the waiting list for a month and I am excited to be a part of this team."

Marty Pavek (to the left of the cake with cap) is honored for his 20 years of service with the Tuesday squad (1996–2016) in August of 2017.

Two years after joining, Aragon has been readily accepted by his team and is sought-after by the squad. He is soft-spoken but garners a lot of attention. He mainly serves as a rifleman but likes every role that he partakes in. "What I love about the squad is the leadership; everyone is treated with respect and fairness and that is really appreciated. No doubt, serving here is the highlight of my week."

Lee Aragon continues, "We had one funeral where a brother and sister came up from Texas and they were the only attendees for that service. The sister came up to us and followed us around to other funerals because she was so touched that we honored her brother. At another funeral, a woman became very emotional; apparently, her father had been a bugler in the military, and she and her family ended up giving an endowment to the rifle squad."

Michael E. Saugen lives in his hometown of Pine Island and drives 66 miles one-way each week to participate with his fellow ex-servicemen. He has been on the Tuesday squad for five years. A Navy man 1967–71, Saugen enlisted right after graduating from Pine Island High and took his basic training at Great Lakes before going to helicopter school in Jacksonville, Florida. He was an E-5 as an aviation ordnance specialist during his four-year stint.

Now 68, Mike saw his first duty in Imperial Beach, California where he was on Sikorski helicopters. Saugen then was aboard the USS *Hornet*, patrolling the Pacific Ocean. Mike was in the Gulf of Tonkin and thus received his Vietnam service medal. A direct but affable sort, Mike is a member of Legion Post 184 in Pine Island. Since joining the Tuesday group in 2012, Saugen has enjoyed rotating roles and relishes all of them, whether presenting, folding the flag, shooting, or parking cars.

"A good friend of mine was buried at the national cemetery out in Sturgis," states Saugen. "I was impressed with that and came out on a Tuesday because that's the day that fit into my schedule. The guys were so accommodating and really helped me learn how to fold the flag properly."

"It's a wonderful detail, and everybody is here for the right reason," adds Saugen. "There is no competition among the guys because the guys have the same focus, to give homage to a fallen comrade. It's a friendly atmosphere, and we're all about giving that last measure of respect to the deceased veteran. It's been the most rewarding experience I've had with a veterans' organization."

A few weeks later, I visit the Tuesday crew for a second time. A freezing rain starts to pelt the almost barren ground and a few minutes later, the snow starts to fall. Upon entering the squad room, the first person I see is Sandy Kleinke, the fellow from Elysian who drives 72 miles one way to reach his volunteer destination each week.

Kleinke points to his car-pooling pal, Ted Zwart, and tells me the roads were a little tricky but they made it here with much time to spare. It's 8:45 a.m., and the first of seven funerals that day will begin at 10:00. Kleinke and Zwart are newcomers to the squad, with their first duty coming in December of 2014. After jokes about who is the better driver, the understated Kleinke is asked about his thought on his brief rifle squad experience as a rifleman.

"I heard about the group from Ted at our Elysian Post 311," says Kleinke. "We got on a waiting list for a year and then got a chance to observe what they do, and I have really enjoyed it." Kleinke served in the U.S. Army 1961–64 as a heavy equipment mechanic and operator and spent some time in Okinawa during his active duty. Following the military stint, Sandy spent his working career in civilian life as a semi-truck driver and a warehouse worker. Originally from Wisconsin, he participated in his local Legion organization there and was on their honor guard for 40 years.

"It's been great to serve the families and to be with the guys," says Kleinke after more than two years on the squad. His commute has shortened, however, now that he is living in Roseville. It's now 17 miles as he drives to White Bear Lake to pick up fellow squad member Jim McGee, who does not drive anymore. After purchasing some doughnuts, they head out to the squad room. "I like being out here so much that there is a good chance I will be volunteering on Fridays, too," Kleinke states.

Ted Zwart grew up on a farm near Edgerton and graduated in 1962. From 1964–70, the former basketball player was in charge of the mess section (food service) as a Sergeant in the Army National Guard. He was stationed at both Pipestone and at Camp Ripley and even did a stint at Fort Knox in Kentucky for six months. Ted worked in construction for 50 years and owned his own building contracting business for 38 years.

"I was at Fort Snelling's cemetery a few times over the years and saw what the rifle squad did," says Zwart. "I also was on the honor guard in Elysian for over 10 years but we only did about one a month. It is so much fun to be around this group of guys, and they have been so willing to help Sandy and me learn."

Right before I move on to another interview, Zwart nudges me and says, "You know, to pay the final honor to these people, the deceased veterans, it's what it's all about. Just last week, the daughter of one of those buried came over to each of us and thanked us, one at a time, for being there for her dad. That really means something to us."

On one of the days I observe the squad, Archie Hazzard offers an interesting story. He was folding a flag for a family and presented it to the widow of the deceased. Unbeknownst to the rest of the family, the widow had requested that the squad not fire the rifles in salute. A few days later, he was informed that there was a complaint about his squad regarding that funeral. Hazzard, who was the Commander that year, stopped by the office and told them, "We don't get complaints." They told him that the children of the deceased had called to complain that the Tuesday squad didn't fire the rifles for their dad. Archie replied, "That's right, we didn't fire the rifles because the wife had requested it and we honored that request."

"When I got home, I called the gentleman who had sent along the complaint," continues Hazzard. "I told him that the widow asked us to not fire the rifles, and he said that the children were unaware of that fact. I asked him if his family could come out the following week at 9:00 a.m. They showed up, and we did the whole thing, including the rifle volleys, for them. It was the right thing to do. The family was crying when I left, and so was I."

Perhaps the saddest days for any of the squads are when they have to perform full military honors for one of their own. When a member of one of the weekdays passes on, it doesn't mean they will be buried on the day that they worked the squad. For Dennis Lande, he will request to be buried on a Tuesday, by his rifle squad mates. "It is so bittersweet, when we have to bury one of our guys. Usually, the family makes a request that the squad their loved one worked on does their honors and so it will be for me," he says.

On a sunny, mild, and windless April morning, there will be nine funerals. Prior to the first one, which will end up with just six people attending, I interview Richard T. Geis. This burly fellow served as the overall Commander of the rifle squads in 2015 and serves on the Fort Snelling Volunteer Committee and as a trustee with the rifle squad. The Farmington resident became a Tuesday team member in 2009 and is active with Legion Post 1776 in Apple Valley. Richard is clearly proud of his participation with the rifle squad and unabashedly states, "It is a pleasure to be here and continue the dedication shown by the men who started this organization. I had it pretty easy in my service, so this is an extension of my military service to the veterans and the community."

"I am a parishioner at the Fort Snelling Chapel," Geis adds. "Ted Nemzek announced that they were looking for members so I came out to the Friday squad to observe and eventually I found a spot on Tuesday. Otherwise, I had no knowledge of the squads. Once you are here, you realize how important the honor guard is to the family. I know that most guys will stay on here until they die."

Geis, 73, is cross-trained in all the roles the squad provides and likes every one of them. He grew up in the Como area of St. Paul and graduated from Murray High School in 1961. From 1966 to 1972, he enlisted in the U.S. Army after being drafted. Richard became a First Lieutenant with the "Honest John" rocket battalion. After training at Fort Sill, Geis recalled reluctantly that they might have been the only unit of the 4th Infantry Division that didn't serve in Vietnam. Instead, he spent most of his service time at Fort Lewis in Washington State. Prior to moving back to Minnesota in 1998, Geis lived in San Diego for 20 years and also in Phoenix and Las Vegas. He spent 20 years as a medical transcriber for Green Hospital of Scripps Clinic and also owned restaurants in his interesting past.

Gerry A. Ballot is a well-versed and confident assistant squad leader for the Tuesday group. Gerry joined the squad in 2008 and currently lives in Stillwater, where he has resided for 23 years and belongs to Legion Post 48. Ballot grew up in northeast Minneapolis and attended De LaSalle High School, graduating in 1965. He matriculated to the University of Minnesota but enlisted in the Army in 1968 and trained at Fort Polk and Fort Sam Houston.

A Sergeant First Class, Ballot was a medic in a hospital unit before becoming the platoon sergeant and chief medical ward officer stateside and was never activated to Vietnam. Following his two years of active duty, Gerry then spent 19 years in the Army Reserve. He was activated during Desert Storm with a mission to increase the number of hospital beds but did not go overseas during that conflict. In civilian life, Ballot was involved in banking, insurance, and commercial real estate; he was a vice president at TCF Bank and also worked for several years for State Farm Insurance.

"When I was at Fort Sam Houston in Texas, I was present at honor guard funerals and they were so impressive," states the low-key Ballot. "I saw a guy once out in Maplewood wearing his rifle squad jacket, and I asked him about it. I have made a lot of great friends out here. For us in the military, it is a real brotherhood and serves a big role in our life. There are a lot of quality people in this group—everybody jokes and has a good time, but we know we are here to do a serious job, to honor the deceased and give tribute to them."

Wayne A. Duerfeldt had to wait two months to join the rifle squad early in 2015, but it was worth it. The Nebraska native and Bloomington resident, now 71, came out on a fall day to observe the squad's machinations and was willing to be patient. Duerfeldt stated, "I had taken a course on the cemetery

The color guard braces against a vicious wind in winter.

put on by Steve Chicoine and was very curious about what they did. It was the first day John Knapp was on the job as the new director of the cemetery, and I heard those rifle volleys, and I was hooked. When I go, I'd like someone do those honors for me, so now is my time to help."

Duerfeldt's dad was in the Navy in WWII, as was his uncle. His brother was in the Air Force. Wayne joined the Army in 1964 and served until 1967; he was a Spec-5 and was in the signal unit with the infantry. He was a combat photographer for 10 months in Vietnam.

A bright man, Duerfeldt must have had no problem graduating from the University of Nebraska with a chemistry degree. He spent his career as a chemist, working for Gould National Battery and then Gopher Resource in Eagan. Wayne belongs to Legion Post 1776 in Apple Valley. An avowed gun expert, he does various roles on the squad but relishes being a rifleman and being a flag-bearer.

Asked about how the funerals affect him, Duerfeldt says,

"I think it's at the smallest funerals when we are affected most because we are there to support this person and there is hardly anyone else present. Once, we had only two people for a service, and the wife of the deceased even followed our bus to the next funeral. We are doing this service not for the veteran but for the family and the loved ones."

"Another time, I was parking cars and a little girl, probably six years old, wearing a summer dress, came up to me and said thank you," adds Duerfeldt. "That was pretty special and something you don't forget. Sometimes, we get people to come on the bus to thank us, too. It is nice to be appreciated."

Dale D. Mallberg is beaming as usual as he scurries around the rifle squad room preparing for 11 funerals on a day with perhaps the first full bloom of spring. It is evident that Dale is a guy comfortable with his place in life and with his role as the assistant squad leader for the Tuesday contingent. Bringing a strong physical presence, Dale was raised in the small farm town of Cogwell, North Dakota. He matriculated to NDSU in Fargo and was in ROTC and came out a 2nd Lieutenant when he joined the Army in 1964.

Mallberg trained at Fort Bliss, Texas, and Fort Benning, Georgia, but he said the best part of his service experience was spending 18 months at Fort Sill, Oklahoma, as a gunnery instructor. For a year, he was in Vietnam as an infantry advisor with a liaison unit to the South Vietnamese. Dale had two uncles in WWII and a brother who was also in Vietnam. He received his combat badge and reached the rank of Captain before finishing his service in 1968.

Now a Maple Grove resident after spending more than 25 years in Plymouth, Mallberg is a member of Legion Post 394 in Hamel. His most prominent job in civilian life was working in inventory control for the Fingerhut Corporation for 17 years. Dale has been volunteering at the Veterans Affairs Medical Center the past 12 years on Thursdays escorting patients and loves every minute of it. Mallberg joined the Tuesday rifle squad in 2006.

"I enjoy the camaraderie of this group so much," remarks the smiling 74-year-old. "It would have been great to have served with all of them in the active military. As for roles on the squad, I like to be the presenter and enjoy the contact with the family at the service. One of the first times I was presenting and we were just about to fold the flag from her father's casket, the daughter of the deceased turned to her other family members and told them that dad really knew how to fold the flag so I hope these guys know what they are doing."

Kent R. Petrie is a kindly 70-year-old with 13 years of service on the Tuesday squad. A 40-year resident of Cottage Grove, Petrie grew up in South St. Paul and graduated from high school in 1965. Both his grandfathers served during WWI, one on a motorcycle battalion and one as a veterinarian tending to the horses with the cavalry. Kent volunteered for the U.S. Army in 1968 at age 20 after going to trade school, and after training at Fort Bragg, North Carolina, he became an E-5 working in psychological services.

During his two years of active duty, Petrie was in Vietnam for seven months and mainly did the preparatory work for the various leaflets that were dropped in Southeast Asia. A reassuring type, Kent adds, "Let's put it this way, it was very interesting work." Upon discharge in 1969, he immediately joined VFW Post 295 in South St. Paul and Legion Post 98 in St. Paul Park.

Upon leaving military service, Petrie went to UW–River Falls on the G.I. Bill of Rights to earn his degree in elementary education. He served with fellow Tuesday squad member Dennis Lande teaching fifth grade for South Washington County schools for 31 years, including 26 at Armstrong Elementary.

His brother's father-in-law, Andy Urness, is on both the Monday and Friday squads and told Petrie about the rifle squads. "I just really like the guys, and that is a big part of being out here," says Petrie, who is cross-trained but likes to be the presenter. "The flexibility we have on this squad is so nice. On the occasion, we have someone from the squad who has a relationship with the deceased, and we allow them to be the presenter and that makes for a really powerful service. Also, our squad leader, Dan Fisher, is very dedicated and very meticulous about everything, and he always makes us look good."

Just as my interview with Petrie comes to a close that early afternoon, Sheryl Osburn climbs aboard the van for an announcement. Sheryl is a volunteer with the Fort Snelling Honor Society. She has been working on Tuesdays for the past nine years and speaks to the family of the deceased immediately following the ceremony. Osburn explains to the squad that there has been a gentleman who has been "hanging around" during most of the day's funerals. She says there is no cause for concern.

To quell any queries or worries, she says she has spoken with the fellow. He is a native of Ukraine and has lived in Chicago for the past few decades. He is at Fort Snelling because he attended a funeral here several years ago and was so impressed with the conduct of the Fort Snelling Memorial Rifle Squad and the condition and ambience of the cemetery itself that he comes out to observe the honor guard funerals whenever he is in the Twin Cities. The squad members are dumbfounded. Really? It's quiet for perhaps five seconds, the assembled squad either shaking or nodding their heads. A whisper in my ear says, "Here I am thinking the guy is a wacko, and he ends up being a true inspiration." Enough said.

Jerome H. Kosel still lives on Inglehart Street in St. Paul, just two blocks from his childhood home. He even married a girl from his neighborhood. Jerry graduated from St. Bernard's High School in 1971 and quickly enlisted in the U.S. Navy, which he said was one of the best things he could have ever done. The Minnesotan was put in charge of the budget for the USS *Decatur*, a guided-missile destroyer. He was an E-5 Second Class Storekeeper. The ship was stationed off Long Beach, California, for two years before spending 13 months off the coast of Vietnam. Following his four-year stint in the Navy, Kosel earned his business degree from the University of Minnesota in 1980.

Possessing a true "servant's heart," Kosel became engaged in community life in Plainview, Minnesota, where he worked for 28 years for State Farm Insurance Company. He has also been a business owner and a certified financial planner. Jerry retired in 2015 and returned to St. Paul; he is a member of Legion Post 39 in North St. Paul. While in Plainview, he was in a local color guard for 20 years, so he was well aware of the honor process. The 64-year-old joined the Friday squad in December of 2016, and while he has been cross-trained, he normally is a flag-bearer. Jerry also serves as an escort on Wednesdays at the Veteran Affairs Medical Center, in addition to teaching low-income people how to budget at the Salvation Army in St. Paul.

Jerry Kosel's father was in George Patton's 3rd Army during WWII and was blown out of a Sherman tank in Africa and was the only survivor of that attack. He is buried at Fort Snelling, as are Jerry's uncle and father-in-law and all of their spouses. Jerry's son-in-law, an Army Ranger, served six years, including a tour in Afghanistan.

"My uncle was buried out here 25 years ago, and I got choked up when they fired the rifle volleys and then played 'Taps' after that," says a grateful Kosel. "After my dad was buried here, too, I just knew then that I wanted to join here eventually. I felt so much pride and respect for what those guys did. I came out and observed with the Tuesday squad and rode with them for a month and found out how things worked. There was room, and I was honored to come on with them. It's just a great crew. It means so much to be a part of this organization."

Terry A. Sventek is a husky but friendly chap who gets

teased a lot by his fellow members and laughs it off like a champ. The chiding means he's liked a lot, of course, in this man's world of constant bantering and continual verbal abuse. Terry grew up in south Minneapolis and graduated from Roosevelt High in 1965 before enlisting in the U.S. Navy at age 18. Sventek trained at the Great Lakes Naval Base near Chicago and served on a destroyer, the USS *Parle*, where he was a gunner's mate and helped to train new recruits.

After his three-year stint as a Seaman, Sventek went to work for Archer Daniels Milling Company on Hiawatha Avenue, not far from his childhood home. Terry was employed there for 30 years and did the gamut of jobs—loading trucks, moving rail cars, carrying 100-pound sacks, serving as a miller, etc. After living in south Minneapolis for 28 years, Sventek has resided in Apple Valley for 20 years and is a member of Legion Post 1776 there. He belongs to the "Grumpy Old Men" 1776 group, a 40-member contingent that does volunteer work for the post.

Terry joined the Tuesday squad in 2006 after some of the guys from the post suggested he join. He's mainly a rifleman but sometimes is a flag-bearer. His father, who was in the Army Air Corps during WWII, is buried at Fort Snelling along with Terry's mother, so he is well aware of the cemetery's meaning. His brother, father-in-law, and, tragically, his 13-year old sister are also interred on the grounds.

"These guys out here are solid people," says the 70-year-old Sventek. "The squad is so professional and everybody knows what to do. It's been a remarkable experience; it took a little while to get adjusted, but I love it."

The entertaining and energetic James J. Heimerl, age 70, flits around like he's still playing defense for the St. Agnes High hockey team. He did play on the ice for the Aggies but also played on the gridiron and the diamond and graduated in the same class as squad leader Dan Fisher in 1965. Jim enlisted in the Marines

Jim Heimerl (right) and Gerry Ballot (left) share a light moment on the van prior to a service.

in February of 1966 and saw plenty of action in Vietnam, as the Lance Corporal was awarded three Purple Hearts.

Heimerl, a good storyteller, relates an incredible occurrence on a hot day in Vietnam in March of 1967. He says, "I had already been wounded twice by that time, and I was sleeping on a jungle trail out in the middle of nowhere. We were so tired, and things were pretty tough at the time. All of a sudden, somebody kicks me in the leg and I jump up, and it's Dan Fisher. I couldn't believe it. Here we are, more than 11,000 miles from home, and there is Dan, my friend and high school classmate. He had been part of a unit that had come in to help us out of danger. He was like my guardian angel, and it really lifted my spirits, when I really needed it."

Jim lives in Medina and is the active Commander of VFW Post 5903 in Hamel. He might be the only person who joined a squad just 24 hours after retirement in January of 2012.

Heimerl was a police officer for 42 years in Minneapolis. For 31 of those years, he was a police lieutenant, establishing a record in city history for the longest tenure in that role. He worked both in north and south Minneapolis; primarily in homicide, narcotics, and robbery.

"At the state fair in 2010, my wife and I run into Dan and his wife at one of the food stands," recalls Heimerl. "He tells me how much he loves being on the rifle squad and that it will be something special for me, too. The next year, believe it or not, we see them at the exact same food stand at the fair. Dan again tells me that he expects to see me out at Fort Snelling right after I retire and on Tuesdays. So, I retired on a Monday and was out there the next morning."

Heimerl and I discuss our love of hockey and the fact we are from large Catholic families. I tell him my wife and I have 152 first cousins between us, and he counters with the fact that his father's family had 14 children and his mother's family had only 13! While he is fun, make no mistake that Jim is dedicated to his cause at Fort Snelling.

"Dan is a caring and compassionate guy, and he has created a real cohesiveness with the Tuesday squad," states Heimerl. "He was one of the smartest kids in our high school class and was always looking out for people and he's still just very kind and professional. There's no doubt that he is the heart and soul of our squad. I know of no other place that I want to be on Tuesdays; I am so happy to out here with these guys and to help give tribute to the families."

On a sun-splashed May morning, Dan Fisher greets me with a broad smile and introduces me to four newer members of the Tuesday squad—Carl Bowman, Lloyd Engler, Ken Erickson, and Brad Nelson.

Carl S. Bowman, a Brooklyn Park resident and a member of Osseo Legion Post 172, immediately radiates a thoughtful and respectful persona and looks much younger than a man of 68. He grew up in North and South Carolina and joined the Army Airborne in 1969 after being drafted. Carl fought in combat in Vietnam for 11 months and was a point-man on patrol, a dangerous proposition. After two years of active duty, Bowman served in the Army Reserve 1972–76. He worked as an Office Manager for the Nash-Finch grocery chain and also for IBM in Rochester.

Bowman commented, "I always wanted to do something in a positive manner when I retired, and I had been on an honor guard at Fort Benning in Georgia. I went to a funeral at the Fort Snelling Chapel and met a chaplain who suggested the rifle squad. Being around guys who went through things similar to what I experienced helps me to deal with internal war wounds."

At this point, Carl starts to get a little emotional as he reaches for his cell phone. He shows me the photo of a young man, Rafael Colon Santos. Bowman goes on to tell me that Santos was just 21 years old when killed in action and that he had taught Carl everything he needed to know about doing the point. "I escorted Rafael's body to Da Nang to the morgue and I give tribute to him every day."

Bowman, who generally serves as a flag-carrier and the carrier of the chrome, is training to shoot the rifle. As he tells me about that, Richard Geis walks by and tells me that Carl is the biggest doughnut eater on the squad. Carl laughs hard. As I thank the likeable fellow for his interview, I get a nudge from a fellow comrade who tells me that Bowman won a Bronze Star for his bravery in Vietnam. Humble, too!

Lloyd B. Engler, a 71-year-old former Army veteran, joined the squad early in 2016 and is a member of Legion Post 580 in Chanhassen. Lloyd graduated from Eden Prairie High School in 1963, when it had a class of just 48 students, and he returned to live in that community for nearly 20 years. Engler's career was in retail management, and he worked for Holiday, Home Depot, and Carpet King over the years.

Engler was drafted in 1968 and became an E-5 personnel specialist. He was in the 199th Light Infantry Brigade and served as a clerk in Vietnam for a year. Working in the casualty section, it was his job to proofread letters sent home to families for those who were killed, wounded, or missing in action.

After reading an article in the paper about the squad and hearing about it from another Tuesday squad member (Lee Aragon), Lloyd decided to come out and take a look. "On my first day observing on Tuesday, we had 15 funerals and Dan let me carry a flag, and that was meaningful," says Engler. "Dan is really good about having all of us learn about all the jobs, but I have mostly done the flags and rifles. I have also done some presenting, and that is very emotional, of course. My wife's cousin was buried here, and I presented for the first time to his wife and that was special. Being with this group is one of the best things I've done in my life."

"People have told us that the honor guard at Fort Snelling was the best part of their funeral service," adds Engler. "In fact, one of the great moments for me came when I was measuring a floor for a new carpet and the man recognized me from the rifle squad. All these guys I serve with are nice guys and some of them can hardly walk, and yet they are still out here serving. It makes you proud."

Ken R. Erickson, who has lived in Eden Prairie for 30 years, heard about the rifle squad from fellow Tuesday members Engler and Aragon and joined in the summer of 2016. The 73-year-old graduated from Minneapolis Washburn in 1961 and then from Hamline University with a history degree in 1965. Erickson served in the U.S. Army 1968–71. After officer candidate school at Fort Benning, Georgia, Ken was a weapons platoon leader at Fort Hood, Texas, and then battalion motor officer as a First Lieutenant in South Korea. His father was in the Army 1925–35.

Erickson, who was trained at Hennepin Country Vocational

Technical, retired from Rosemount Engineering after 23 years as a computer programmer and is a member of Legion Post 580 in Chanhassen. The soft-spoken gentleman remarks, "I knew Lee and Lloyd, of course, and they encouraged me to join them. I had always wanted to do something special to honor our veterans. I didn't serve in combat, so I feel I owe it to those who did. Even though I had served, emotionally I feel that my service was not equal to theirs."

"I've heard some amazing stories since I came on about some of the funerals," says Erickson. "One time, a guy on a bicycle actually rode through the formation that was established for the ceremony." Ken just shakes his head and walks away.

Paul B. Nelson and I hit it off immediately, probably because it's apparent he is a stand-up guy and because we are just months apart in age. All three boys in his family were called by their middle name, so he is known as Brad. Nelson is still in great physical condition at the age of 64. He belongs to VFW Post 1782 in White Bear Lake, where he resides. He joined the squad in July 2016 after retiring from a career in accounting; the last five he spent with the St. Paul school system after years working with non-profit organizations.

Nelson grew up in south Minneapolis and graduated from Washburn in 1970. His draft lottery number of 348 meant he was in no danger to be drafted into the military. Although his dad was a Marine who served during WWII, his parents weren't pleased when he enlisted in the Army in February of 1972. Resolute, he says, "Joining the Army was the best thing that ever happened to me. I spent three years in Germany in the Signal Corps, mostly as a company clerk."

Not finished with the military yet, Nelson served in the Army Reserve 1976–82 and then the National Guard 1982–86 before again finishing up with the Army Reserve 1988–2004. In total, he spent 27 years in military service. In his final year, he worked in Iraq in logistics. Brad retired as a Lieutenant Colonel.

Color guard and rifle squad ready themselves for the morning's first funeral.

In 1967, Brad's oldest brother, Carter, was killed in action in Vietnam. The First Lieutenant was piloting an Air Force Phantom jet when he was shot down. Nelson states, "It was hard to take that news. I knew I wouldn't have to be going to Vietnam because of his death. Being on the rifle squad is one of the ways I can honor Carter. He is buried here, and I remember the Air Force honor guard that came from North Dakota. I knew both Richard Geis and Ted Stamos from Tuesday, and I started thinking about joining a few years before I retired."

On a hot and humid summer day, it was pleasure to interview two guys born a few months apart in 1946—Rick Clifton and Jim Pagel. Richard L. Clifton has lived in West St. Paul for 30 years but was raised in South St. Paul and graduated in 1964. Rick was drafted into the U.S. Army in 1965 and trained as an infantry "grunt." He took his jungle training at Fort Lewis, Washington, and recalls the replication of a Vietnamese village as astounding for its accuracy to the real thing.

In his third month fighting in Vietnam as a grenade-launcher, he was wounded and spent three months rehabbing in a Japanese hospital before being deployed again in Vietnam for six months as a perimeter guard and medical transporter. He goes on to tell me that he got a kiss from bombshell Joey Heatherton during one of Bob Hope's USO shows in Vietnam. He says that she told him he was "real cute" and planted a big wet one on him.

"After active service, I switched from one national uniform to another," giggles Clifton. "I became a letter-carrier for the U.S. Postal Service and did that for 30 years, mostly in Roseville." Rick retired in 2001 and joined the rifle squad the next year. Now 71, Clifton is a member of VFW Post 295 in South St. Paul and has mainly served as a rifleman and bus driver over the past 15 years at Fort Snelling.

"Joe Conley was on the squad and he was a friend of mine," remembers the upright Clifton. "He simply told me that I would be coming out to join them when I retired. We were shorthanded at the time, and I became the youngest guy on the squad. I never want to miss a week out here, and I wouldn't trade it for anything. My life revolves around my Tuesday volunteering, and it's very important for me to repay my fellow veterans. We try to be as professional as we can be for the families."

James L. Pagel is a stand-up guy from Cannon Falls. He has lived almost his entire life there, graduating from high school in 1964. Pagel did three years of active duty (1964–67) with the Marine Corps and was involved in heavy combat in Vietnam while "in country" for 13 months as a radio operator and machine-gunner. Jim, a quick study, finished his tour as a Sergeant E-5; he had the somewhat rare distinction of serving with all three Marine divisions: the 1st Marines (2nd battalion) at Camp Pendleton, the 2nd Marines (2nd battalion) at Camp Lejuene, and the 3rd Marines (9th battalion) in Vietnam.

Following his discharge, the young Minnesotan went to Control Data's electronics school and then was employed by

Univac for a few years before moving on to 3M. From 1975 to 2009, Pagel worked for the U.S. Postal Service, as did Clifton; he spent the final 25 years as a postmaster in Welch, Kenyon, and Goodhue.

Jim is a member of VFW Post 4452 in Cannon Falls and joined the Tuesday crew shortly after his retirement in 2009. Just turned 71, he rotates among several roles on the squad, likes them all, and does whatever he is asked by squad leader Dan Fisher.

"We go out to serve and don't care what we do," remarks Pagel. "I love being out there with the guys. When I came out, I didn't have a clue what I was getting into, but we had a bunch of older guys who we always looked up to, like Leon Simon, and they treated us well. Now we have a good group of younger guys, and it's a nice mix."

Through all the ceremonies, one stands out for Pagel; it was the service for former squad member Bernie Melter, a good friend of Jim's and also a resident of Cannon Falls. It was in late November of 2015 and Pagel was the flag presenter on that solemn day. Melter had been the one to get Jim out volunteering with the rifle squad.

"I had talked to Bernie and told him I would be retiring later in the week on a Friday," states Pagel. "He picked me up on the next Tuesday, and I was on the squad. Now, here I was presenting the flag to his wife, Midge, and it was emotional. Ted Stamos, another former Tuesday member, did a great job setting up that service as we had the Patriot Guard out and a fly-over, too. There was a great outpouring of support from the other day's squads as a sign of respect for Bernie."

Chapter 7

Friday Squad

On yet another cold winter day in mid-February, a visit to the Memorial Rifle Squad room attached to the Fort Snelling National Cemetery maintenance facility leads to a morning of meeting more members of this exemplary organization. Already present is 89-year-old George Weiss, Jr., the original founder and the Friday squad leader for the past 38 years. Though he isn't in uniform, he's already arranging the lineup for the day's funerals. Because of a recent illness that led to his hospitalization, Weiss was driven to the cemetery by his grandson, Jeremy.

Phil Tryke and Ernie Denzer are busy cleaning their Springfield 03 rifles in the back room of the squad's area in preparation for their rifle duties. Tryke, a very helpful gentleman, had picked up the day's lunch and jokes that he is the "mess cook" for the Friday group. A Minneapolis native and a 1958 Henry High graduate, Tryke was in the Navy 1959–65 and served as a jet engine mechanic. He was with a fighter squadron on a carrier in the Pacific. He tells me, "During the Cuban Missile Crisis, we were right off the coast of Russia and we were fully loaded; I don't think people know how close to nuclear war we were."

After serving as a pipefitter for 37 years, the 77-year-old Plymouth resident joined the rifle squad in 2006 and has been

Ken Gibson (left) and Ernie Denzer (right) fold the flag in preparation for a Friday.

a member of VFW Post 1286 in Bloomington. Tryke, who normally is a rifleman, adds, "My dad, who is buried out here at Fort Snelling along with other relatives, didn't get the military honors he deserved, and that motivated me to become a part of this organization. It is quite fulfilling to be here for the families. It can be very moving. In the end, the few minutes we spend with them may be moments that they remember forever."

Ernest J. Denzer, Jr., a well-spoken resident of Minnetonka, joined the squad in 2013 after a long career in the IT field. A Le Sueur native, the 66-year old worked for many years with Carlson Companies and Express Scripts after earning a business degree from the University of Minnesota. A year after retiring, he decided to join the rifle squad after being recruited by a friend who gave a presentation on the rifle squad at his Legion Post 450 in St. Paul. Ernie was in supply and personnel during his service in the Army Reserves 1971–1993, most of it served at Fort Snelling. In 1991, he was called to active duty during the Gulf War and served overseas in Saudi Arabia.

It is clear that after four years on the Friday squad Denzer has great admiration for his senior compatriots. He says, "We have several guys in their 80s and 90s on this squad and their dedication is amazing. Some of them are as old as my parents, and they are here every week. We are here to honor the veterans and their families, and they need to know that we care. At these funerals, we are honoring someone who has served our nation, and everybody is the same, no matter what they did while they were serving. What is really significant is that all the gravestones are the same, no matter your rank or what service you were in or whether or not you were decorated."

In the midst of a game of cribbage, 90-year-old Charlie Korlath sticks out his hand for an introduction. Born and raised in St. Paul, the affable fellow with a silver moustache is quick with a witticism for a couple of Marines giving him a bad time about his service choice. Korlath has been on the Friday squad for 36 years and belongs to VFW Post 4462 and Legion Post 533, both in St. Paul. Charlie enlisted in the Navy in 1944 before graduating from Monroe High School. He spent four years as a gunner's mate while serving on a troop transport in the Pacific.

The garrulous Korlath spent almost two years in China, mostly in Shanghai and Tsingtao. I mention that my father was also in the Navy at that time and was also in those two cities, and I joke that perhaps they had a beer together sometime during their WWII stint. Charlie shares several photos he took on September 2, 1945, the day of the official Japanese surrender in Tokyo Bay. Sure enough, there are pictures of the USS *Missouri* and also of scenes at Yokohama Harbor.

It is readily apparent that Korlath relishes the camaraderie of his group. He started with George Weiss as his squad leader for the Friday squad in May of 1981, and he has been the assistant squad leader as long as he can remember. In 1986 he was the Commander, and he spent 28 years as the finance officer for the rifle squad. As a civilian, Charlie spent more than 30 years as a firefighter for the city of St. Paul. Generally, he was the driver of a hook and ladder. On this day, Korlath will present the American flag to the family after each funeral. By his estimation, he has been the presenter to more than 19,000 families over his tenure. Imagine that!

"I figure that the Friday squad has done about 30% of the overall funerals over the years," says the razor-sharp Korlath. "When I present, I try to look into the eyes of the person who

Charlie Korlath, who joined the rifle squad in 1981, has presented approximately 19,000 flags to families over the years.

is receiving the flag, and I try to help them out as much as I can. Sometimes, it is difficult to get out all the words we speak to them because they are so overwhelmed, but we know that they appreciate what we are doing for them."

"I have known George Weiss for more than 40 years," says the good-natured Korlath about the founder. "We were in the same Legion Post (6210, St. Paul) for many years when he was the district commander, and George just told me I would be going on the rifle squad when I retired and that's what happened. He is definitely a 'gung-ho' kind of guy and there is no doubting that he is tough, but he can also be a lot of fun. I always got along with him but I could holler at him, too."

There are 15 volunteers for this day's responsibilities. Though it is 15° above, a strong 20-mile-per-hour wind from the north makes it brisk and raw, with occasional snow. The volunteers are dressed appropriately for the day but one has to steady himself against the wind as he boards the van. One of the fellows walks alongside me and says with a straight face, "I'm in the witness-protection program, so you won't be able to get my name." After a few seconds, we both burst out laughing. I reply, "Thanks, Mr. Barnes, I'll catch you in the van." It's John Barnes, a fellow always ready with a one-liner.

Jesse Montez, a proud Mexican-American who served in the Marines, deftly fends off a barb from Korlath. Astounded to find out he's 86 years old, I tell him he could easily pass for 65. A quick smile comes across his face and he goes on to tell me about his Hispanic community in West St. Paul. He quit school at age 14 in 1946 to work for Cudahay's, a meat-packing plant in Newport. After working as a laborer there, he signed up to join the Marines and was on active duty 1951–53 but to his regret, he never served in Korea. Instead, he was stateside at Camp Pendleton.

Montez was in the Marine Reserves for another six years while starting his 30-year career as a laborer in the machine shop and as a butcher at Armour's in South St. Paul. A diminutive man, Montez has a quiet confidence about him and relishes his role on the color guard carrying the chrome rifle. Jesse tells me that I must come to his long-time church, Our Lady of Guadalupe, to have enchiladas. He tells me he has been a member there since he was a kid and that his grandfather, Alberto, helped start the church. Later, he nudges me to inform me that his grandfather fought in the Spanish-American War.

"I had some friends from my post tell me about the rifle squad, and I told them I would join for two years just to shut them up," says a grinning Montez, who has a brother and an uncle interred at Fort Snelling. "Now, I've been here for 12 years and I don't intend to ever leave. I just like being with the good guys here." Montez served on the Friday squad with his brother-in-law Jesse Arias for nine years before Jesse died in 2015.

After I finished with Montez, Ernie Denzer introduces me to Quentin DeNio, another legendary figure among the Fort Snelling Memorial Rifle Squad volunteers. DeNio was born in Cedar Rapids, Iowa, on September 10, 1919, the same year the Treaty of Versailles was signed to officially end World War I. It was the same year that Babe Ruth hit 29 homers for the Red Sox and just before he was sold to the New York Yankees. His right hand envelops mine and it is vice-like. DeNio might be 96 but he's still sharp as a tack. Told that I am writing a book about the rifle squad, he quickly replies, "These other guys come out every week to see if I've died." The dozen or so men gathered by now all laugh in unison.

Quentin DeNio is the oldest member of the rifle squad volunteers. Yet, he didn't join until he was 80 years old. It is clear right away that he is a humble and unassuming man. DeNio, a resident of south Minneapolis, belongs to VFW Post 5555 and Legion Post 435 in Richfield. He has been a member of the American Legion in Richfield for 70 years. Quentin joined the U.S. Army in 1941 and served through 1945 as an infantryman. He saw 42 months of combat in some of the fiercest battles in the Central Pacific, including Saipan and Eniwetok (which became the first island where the U.S. could land B-17s). He was in the famous battle of Okinawa. Queried about his combat duty, all he says is, "The worst thing that happened to me in WWII was that the Japanese shot my radio antenna off as I had it up to my ear."

Following the war, DeNio went to Dunwoody Institute and got into the printing business. He owned his own print shop (DeNio Designs) on Lake Street for over 35 years. His shop made invitations, announcements, and envelopes. Quentin retired in 1994.

This day, DeNio is a flag-carrier, and he is the one specified to carry the particular service flag the deceased served in while in the military. I watch him steady the flag in the 20-mile-per-hour gusts amidst the spit of sleet, shake my head, and think, "These guys really are something." Here is a guy 96 years old and he's out here every week, battling the elements to serve. After rolling up his flag, Quentin accepts a little help to get back in the van and settles among his brethren.

"Our Legion Post in Richfield used to have an honor squad, and I belonged to that for quite a few years, but only two of us were left so I came out to Fort Snelling," says DeNio. "I think the most meaningful days are the ones when we're the only ones here for the deceased."

After I finish interviewing DeNio, several others stop by to mention something about him, and it's obvious they adore the man.

Quentin DeNio stands holding the Navy flag at a funeral in 2016, his final year on the Friday squad at age 96.

Al Moller says, "Quentin is an inspiration to all of us and we all look up to him. Can you imagine, he spent three and a half years in the Pacific fighting with no leave, and he survived three amphibious assaults on Japanese-controlled islands?" Tim Gabrio remarks, "He is just a very special man; I and all the others from the Friday squad get hand-written notes from him all the time." Later, a guy whispers to me, "You know that he got the Bronze Star, don't you?" Well, no, he didn't mention that, but it doesn't surprise me. By the summer of 2017, DeNio was inactive and in an assisted living arrangement. He was getting so many visits from his comrades on the rifle squad that his roommate requested a room change!

John Barnes, a 68-year-old quipster from Richfield who belongs to the VFW Post 5555 there, serves as a rifleman. He grew up in south Minneapolis and graduated from St. Louis Park High School in 1967. John enlisted in the Navy right out of high school and served four years as a petty officer on submarine duty. His home station was New London, Connecticut, the home of the Coast Guard Academy. Barnes's submarines perused the Atlantic Coast, from Halifax in Canada down to Puerto Rico. After a 20-year career building walk-in coolers and freezers, Barnes then started another 20-year career making signs.

"I just love being on the Friday squad," says Barnes, who started on the squad in 2013. "I can't say I like the cold weather, but it's our job and we're here no matter what the conditions are. The first time I witnessed the squad was when my father-in-law died and when we were out to Fort Snelling for the burial, there was a blinding blizzard. Driving out here, we couldn't even see the tombstones. I remember that we could barely make out the rifle squad in the blizzard, but there they were, and I thought that was really something."

Greg Rollinger, who is serving as the squad leader this day, joined the rifle squad in 2008 after retiring from a career in computer software and programming with both Pillsbury and Honeywell. He spent 15 years with each of those Twin Cities pillars. Greg grew up in White Bear Lake and attended Hill High School and graduated in 1966, before it merged with Murray, the Catholic girls' school, shortly thereafter. Rollinger was drafted into the U.S. Army and served 1968–70 and says that he was in Vietnam for exactly 365 days, no more or no less. He was a buck Sergeant in the infantry and was an M-16 machine-gunner, serving as a squad leader with the 4th Division in the Central Highlands.

The Friday squad photographed near Committal Shelter 4 in August 2017.

Now 68, Rollinger gives off the aura of a leader—quiet, strong, and direct. He normally serves as a rifleman but takes over the job of squad leader when Weiss or assistant squad leader Gene Schultz is not present or able. He was the overall commander in 2012. Greg is a member and former commander of VFW Post 9433 in Rosemount, where he resided for many years; he now lives in Inver Grove Heights. He had been very active with the VFW but was looking for new opportunities to serve. Accessing the Internet, he found the rifle squad and sent an e-mail to long-time Friday member Ted Nemzek. He didn't know much about the squad, but soon he was out to observe for three or four weeks and joined up.

Just as the volunteer group steps out for another honor guard presentation, 68-year-old Joe Collova strolls over with his bugle. A peppy and jovial type, Collova waits as long as he can before venturing out to do "Taps." A 1962 graduate of St. Paul Monroe, Joe still lives in the capital city and belongs to VFW Post 4462 in West St. Paul and the Marine Corps League. He enlisted in the Marine Corps in 1967 and served his four-year stint; the Sergeant was a truck driver and an administrative assistant. For 13 months, he did duty in Vietnam.

Collova, who worked as a printer for the city of St. Paul and Ramsey Country for a total of 33 years, remarks, "I had seen the segment on WCCO featuring the Friday squad, and they were looking for people, so I was lucky to be able to join right away, and I have been bugling with Tom Mullon ever since. I also play "Taps" for other funerals outside Fort Snelling and at nursing homes and in small towns in northern Minnesota."

"We have a lot in common as individuals with our service experiences," add Collova. "We all have the same simple goal: to honor those who served our country in whatever fashion they did so. It is a privilege to be able to serve under George Weiss, who has done an exceptional job putting the squads together; he is highly respected and can be so proud of the tradition of excellence they have established."

The friendly and articulate Al Moller sits across from me in the van and regales me with information about the Friday squad. He seems to know a lot about both the military careers and the personal lives of all of his mates. Al has been suffering with some respiratory issues so he rarely ventured out of the van on this cold morning, but he serves as a great source of information. Al graduated from Bemidji High School in 1960 and enlisted in the Navy right away at age 17, serving four years of active duty as a machinist's mate before joining the Navy Reserves for another three years. He trained in Guantanamo Bay and was in the Atlantic and Caribbean Sea during the tense days of the Cuban Missile Crisis.

Like Phil Tryke, Moller was a long-time pipefitter before becoming an assistant business manager of the local union. In all, he spent 42 years in the business. Now residing in Farmington, Al is a member of VFW Post 9433 in Rosemount and Legion Post 594 in Eagan but also belongs to the Fleet Reserve Association and the Disabled American Vets. He also volunteers at the Veterans Affairs Hospital in Minneapolis. He remarks, "I am proud to be a Navy veteran and proud to be on this memorial squad." Moller's wife made some white cotton cloth scarves with classy gold lettering on them for the Friday squad that add a special touch to their winter garb.

Tim Gabrio drives the van on the first of my visits to the Friday squad without any mishaps but still takes some not-so-gentle chiding from his squad-mates for the back steps scratching on the road as we make our way to another funeral stop. Gabrio is just 63 years old, one of the youngest of the rifle squad members, but he served as overall Commander in 2009. Yet another St. Paulite, he graduated from Johnson in 1969 and later lived in St. Paul and Lino Lakes before settling in Hugo for the past six years. He spent 30 years in the printing business, mostly as a manager in the bindery. However, he is one of the rare volunteers who started duty on the squad while he was still working full-time.

"I worked long days Monday through Thursday so I was free on Fridays," said Gabrio, an enlisted Navy man 1969–73 who was in helicopter support and spent a year in Vietnam. "I worked four days a week at my job and then came out here for three years before I retired. It worked out nicely for me. My father-in-law was buried out here, and they had a pamphlet about the squad, so I knew then that I wanted to do this and it's been everything I expected. To me, we have the honor of burying someone that we might consider a special friend."

Back at the squad room for lunch, one of the older volunteers sidles up to me and quietly murmurs, "I'm 100% Irish and damn proud of it—my mother's family is from Tipperary and my father's side is from Kilkenny—have you ever heard of those places?" Certainly, I concur, and introduce myself. He is one Edward P. (Kevin) Burns, a real charming character with a very subtle wit. He's got stories, of course, that only an Irishman can tell, but he's also intuitive and perceptive.

Kevin's self-deprecating humor is disarming but I must pay strict attention to what he is saying. He is 93 years old and in a month will turn 94. Once again, I am stunned by yet another veteran's recall and insight. He apologizes for his hearing deficit and the weakness in his voice. Burns grew up out East and served in the Marine Corps 1942–46. He was a tank driver and then commander of a tank unit and saw plenty of action in the Pacific during WWII. He regales me with factoids about combat in the Marshall Islands and how he was shot out of five tanks but survived them all.

Kevin Burns got into that fledgling new enterprise called television after the war. He started out in Pittsburgh and ventured to Minnesota in 1965 to work for WCCO-TV. He ended up spending 50 years in the business, mostly as a cameraman. He finally retired in 1994. I ask him about the noteworthy names from WCCO, and he has a positive thing to say about each of them.

A member of the Marine Corps League, the USMC Council, and the Disabled American Veterans, Burns joined the rifle squad in 1986 after a fellow Marine named John O'Neill told him he had to join. O'Neill, who was involved in a number of veteran organizations, was on the Friday squad and so Burns joined on. Soon, Burns also joined the Tuesday squad and showed up for duty twice a week for over 20 years. He also served as overall Commander of the rifle squad in 1995.

"The people who come to serve here are extremely dedicated," says Burns—an understatement, no doubt. "To me, it's one of the most honorable things a veteran can do." Burns, by the way, had his first parachute jump at the age of 92!

Joe Starr was in the Navy 1964–67 after growing up in Willmar. He joined several others on the Friday squad as new recruits in August of 2014 and has adjusted well to his new surroundings. Starr's role is to carry the American flag. Joe belongs to the Richfield Legion Post 535 and to Lake Street VFW Post 246 in Minneapolis and the Golden Valley Legion Post. He was a gunner's mate on an LST in two tours of Vietnam as he scoured the rivers and waterways. He relishes the ship's reunions every two years that take place around the nation.

"About 30 years ago, I lost two good friends. They were buried out here and the rifle squad did the services, and I was so impressed," says Starr, who resides in nearby Bloomington. "I waited two years and finally got to join, and it has exceeded my expectations. Besides respecting our deceased at the funerals, it is amazing to see the dedication to the cause these guys have. I really get a kick out of some of these guys."

The first time I visited the Friday crew, a few years ago, it was a clear and cold February morning. There are only about 10 volunteers gathered, which was fortunate, perhaps, as there were just four funerals on the docket. Founder and squad leader George Weiss arrived with his grandson Jeremy and was soon giving instructions to observer and possible new recruit Tony Thompson in his direct and authoritative manner.

Thompson made sure he was on time for his first day observing the Friday squad, and he remarked to me that he was really hoping they would decide to add him to the group. Tony grew up in Minneapolis and graduated from Southwest High in 1966. After being drafted, he enlisted in the U.S. Navy and served 1968–72 as a boiler technician. The petty officer had Pearl Harbor as his home port for most of his active duty. On a destroyer-escort in the Pacific, his ship covered the entire ocean during his stint and they patrolled the area surrounding Vietnam, especially the Tonkin Gulf.

Thompson, an Osseo resident, belonged to the Palmer-Lake Legion Post in Brooklyn Center. He had been aware of the reputation of the rifle squad for years and told me he always had a desire to serve on it. Thompson joined the Northwest Metro wing of the Patriot Guard in 2014. His civilian career included 11 years working as security guard for the U.S. Federal Courthouse as a marshal and 25 years as a sergeant in Internal Affairs for Hennepin County. A respectful man whose sincerity is readily apparent, Thompson told me that frigid morning, "I am so looking forward to being a part of this noteworthy group, to do my part. My father-in-law, a Seabee in World War II, was buried out here at Fort Snelling, and so will I."

Two years later, Thompson is now 69 and is clearly settled in his role on the squad. On this day, he is carefully folding flags with Ken Gibson and Ernie Denzer. I tell him that he looks pretty comfortable, and he acknowledges with a wink and a broad smile. "It's been an honor to be out here as a member, and that word truly sums it up for me," he remarks. "I still get goose bumps when 'Taps' is played, as you never get used to it."

Soon after, I interview a fellow named Jack Wallace, a former Army medic who served 1969–71. Included in his military duty was 18 months spent in Vietnam. A native of Boston, Jack has lived in Rosemount for the past 37 years. After working at a VA Hospital in Boston for a year as a medical assistant, he came to Minnesota to partake in the physician's assistant program at the Minneapolis VA, and he spent four years in that job after finishing the two-year training period.

He belongs to Legion Post 65 and VFW Post 9433 in his adopted city and has been a member of the Friday squad for about six months. Wallace retired in 2013 after spending 27 years with the Minnesota State Patrol, exclusively spent in the Twin Cities metro area.

"It's quite an eclectic group of guys out here," remarks the self-effacing Wallace. "They are all interesting guys in their own way, and I love being around them and listening to their stories and about their life experiences. I knew assistant squad leader Greg Rollinger from my Rosemount group, and I got on a waiting list and am glad to finally be on the squad. Perhaps part of the reason for joining up was some survivor-guilt I have from my war experience—I am here to help for those I couldn't help back in Vietnam."

Wallace isn't new to honoring veterans. For the past 25 years, he served on a color guard for his Rosemount Legion. The 68-year-old also worked for many years to put flags on the graves of veterans in Rosemount and Apple Valley. Jack also works security at Target Field.

After finishing a game of cribbage, Mike Pluta saunters over with a hearty smile and a handshake. He is rifle squad royalty, so to speak. His father, Lawrence, was one of the co-founders in 1979, and Mike was part of only the second father-and-son combination to volunteer for the squad. Dennis (father) and Don (son) Christy are the other pair to be two-generation family members.

Lawrence Pluta was a career Navy man, but he died of lung cancer in 1995 and is buried at Fort Snelling. The military life runs deep in the Pluta family, as Mike's sister Patricia became a Master Chief in the U.S. Navy in a 22-year career. Mike's grandfather, also named Lawrence, was in the Navy in WWI. The personable Pluta joined the Friday squad in 2011.

Growing up on West 7th Street in St. Paul, Mike Pluta played football at North St. Paul and graduated in 1965. However, his military career started prior to his graduation. Influenced by his father, Mike signed up for the Navy Reserves in his junior year. He spent a weekend a month at Wold Chamberlain and then went on active duty 1965–67. Pluta was stationed on the USS *Ranger*, an aircraft carrier, and he was on the fight control team moving the planes in position for take-off. He had one tour of duty in Vietnam in 1966, routinely patrolling between that embattled country and the Philippines. He also spent a year based in Bremerton, Washington. As a civilian, Pluta first worked as a meat-cutter but then spent most of his career in middle management selling meat for Applebaum's and Rainbow Foods.

A classy and astute guy, Pluta has worked every aspect of the rifle squad since his retirement in 2009. He is a member of VFW Post 295 in South St. Paul, where he lives, and also

Mike Pluta (back), assistant squad leader, is set to command the rifle squad.

is a member of the Fleet Reserve Association 136 in Crystal. He looks at least a decade younger than his age of 69, and his enthusiasm and affection for his mates is strong.

"When I retired, I was either going to volunteer at the VA Hospital in Minneapolis or with the rifle squad," says a sincere Pluta. "I first tried to join the Tuesday squad because that was the day that my dad volunteered, but there wasn't any room, so Archie Hazzard told me that George Weiss would really like to have me serve with him on Fridays so that's what I did. I am so proud to be among these guys to do what we do. Someday, I will be buried here, no doubt."

"The toughest thing to deal with being on the squad is having to work a service for one of your comrades on the squad," says Pluta. "We have had to do that two times, and that was really difficult. I have spent some time presenting the flag to the family and that is pretty powerful and emotional, too. In fact, there have been times when I have had to re-say the wording of our devotion because I got choked up."

On a beautiful early May morning, the grounds at the cemetery are immaculate and a brilliant emerald as I saunter toward the squad room for another round of interviews. Sadly, there are several gentlemen who are not present, due to death, illness, or physical limitations. However, it's time to meet some of the newer members.

There are 14 funerals on this day and the guys are talking about seven so-called "doubles"—husband and wife combination burials. They are really excited when George Weiss announces that the last service of the day would actually be a true "double" as both the husband and wife had served, and that the squad would indeed conduct a separate service for each of them. There was a genuine buzz of excitement in the room.

Following a few instructions from assistant squad leader Mike Pluta, the assembled members ready their rifles for the day's shooting, slam down a few doughnuts, or get back to their card games. Andy Urness, the unassuming former Navy veteran who also volunteers on Mondays (see chapter 9), plays cribbage with Charlie Korlath, Phil Tryke, and Kevin Burns. Ken Gibson, who also doubles up on Mondays and Fridays with Urness, is busy preparing the ammunition for the day.

Meanwhile, I walk toward a guy who is a dead ringer for former baseball pitcher Jack Morris. I recognize him from the last few Memorial Day events—it's Bob Selden, who has been the master of ceremonies for Memorial Day services in recent years. Selden grew up close to Fort Snelling, having been raised in Bloomington. He was a Lincoln graduate in the class of 1968 and spent 20 years in the Air Force (1971–90).

Bob spent time in Minot, North Dakota, as well as in New Jersey, Mississippi, Arizona, Washington, D.C., and Iceland. In the final 12 years of active duty, he was in communications management, code-speak for setting up and commanding major international events. Selden assisted the Secret Service in the 1980, 1984, and 1988 presidential campaigns.

Selden worked for 20 years as a field engineer for Industrial Television Services before joining the rifle squad in February of 2017. Perhaps no one was as knowledgeable about the rifle squads prior to joining than Selden, who has now been the master of ceremonies for Memorial Day for four years and has been the president of the Fort Snelling Volunteer Committee, which coordinates the Memorial Day services and is primarily made up of members of the Memorial Rifle Squad.

"I absolutely love being on the squad," states Selden. "These guys are great; I've known a lot of the Friday guys for a while so that's why I chose this day. What surprises me is the large number of funerals; as the last day of the week, it seems like we are always having 15–17 each day." In addition to his service at Fort Snelling each week, Selden works significant hours in the Masonic Fraternity.

A resident of Roseville for over 25 years, Selden is a member of Legion Post 542 there and of the Legion of Honor at Zurah Shrine in St. Paul. He learned rifle commands for those two organizations' honor guards, so it's natural that his role for the Friday squad is to be a rifleman.

"Being on the volunteer committee here at Fort Snelling for about 10 years gave me an opportunity to learn a lot about the squads," adds Selden. "I knew I would join right away after retiring from my full-time job, and it's a good fit for me. No question about it, I will be buried out here, too."

Thorne S. Helgesen, 64, grew up in Minneapolis but went to high school in Garden Grove, California. Tony, as he is known, now lives in Woodbury and belongs to VFW Post 9024 there after living in Maple Grove for 15 years. Helgesen enlisted in the Army in 1971 and was a military policeman for his three-year stint. Tony spent an entire year in Vietnam, and although he was based in Saigon, he flew all over the country by helicopter.

Helgesen joined the Friday team in the summer of 2015 after a long career in law enforcement. Tony was a Fridley police officer for several years before spending 17 years as a detective for the Anoka County Sheriff's Department. He has done everything on the squad except being a rifleman. Tony most enjoys telling the family how the ceremony is going to be conducted and then assisting with folding the flag.

"I was out to the cemetery for the funeral of my cousin a few years ago," states Helgesen. "It happened to be the Friday squad, and I was impressed with what transpired. I came out to observe and I got on right away. For me, carrying the remains of the cremated deceased is a big honor and I value it highly."

"I knew most of the guys would be older," continued Tony. "However, I was really surprised at the longevity of some who were still out here, some for well over 30 years. Once you join, nobody wants to leave unless they die or are too sick or frail to participate. It is true dedication. I feel so proud to be able to do this and to know that I will be buried here someday, too."

Tony and I commiserate about being the same age, and he introduces me to yet another 64-year-old, also a Woodbury resident, named Robert A. Hjelmen. Bob is a straightforward fellow who was also in law enforcement. Hjelmen was a detention officer for 25 years with the Otter Tail Sheriff's Department and retired in 2012. Like Helgesen, he joined the Friday squad in 2015.

After growing up in Grand Forks, North Dakota, and graduating from Central High, Bob took a delayed enlistment into the U.S. Army at age 19 after receiving the #7 lottery number. On active duty 1972–74, Hjelmen was in the infantry and served for two years in Germany, near Stuttgart. Following his military career, he moved to Fergus Falls, where he lived for 32 years. He is a member of Legion Post 501 in Woodbury.

"I saw a news article on the rifle squads and sent an e-mail to Mike Pluta of the Friday squad," said Hjelmen. "They had an opening. I came out and observed and was accepted into the squad. I always wanted to honor the veterans in this way. It's nice to come together for the same cause. I have been quite surprised about the tremendous variety in the occupations the guys were involved in with their civilian careers. One of the things I like best is that we keep tabs on the guys who are retired or inactive, showing concern for their welfare for all they have done for the squad."

Wayne Kopesky graduated from Eden Prairie High in 1963 when the now-burgeoning school had but 38 seniors. A resident of Bloomington since 1976 and a member of VFW Post 1296 in that city, Kopesky was accepted onto the Friday squad early in 2016. Wayne's father was a Marine, and he fought on Guadalcanal, Iwo Jima, and Okinawa during WWII.

Wayne enlisted in the U.S. Army in 1969. After officer-training school in engineering, he went to airborne and military intelligence school. Kopesky, now 71, was sent to Vietnam in 1970 and spent a year in country with the 509th Radio Research group in reconnaissance. He completed his reserve duty as a Major. In his civilian life thereafter, Kopesky taught for a few years in Iowa before moving back to Minnesota to teach physics and chemistry at Minneapolis South.

"We take turns doing different assignments on the squad, but I really enjoy holding the Army flag," says Kopesky, a polite chap. "I look forward to every Friday and have made some great friends. We all need to be a part of something outside of ourselves, and it feels good to give homage to people as they are laid to their final rest."

Undoubtedly the youngest member of any of the weekday rifle squad's is Stephen J. Rada, who is 55. Rada joined the Marine Corps at age 18 in 1980 and became an LVTP-7 crew chief and was involved with logistics for his four-year stint. Steve spent 23 years as a corrections officer at the Stillwater prison. Currently, Rada is a math and English tutor at Central Park Elementary in Roseville, where he has resided for the past 26 years and belongs to Legion Post 542. Steve joined the Friday group in November of 2016.

"I'm not ashamed to say I get teared up at the funerals," says a steely-eyed Rada. "It is great sorrow to see people crying during the ceremonies. It is both rewarding and sad at the same time. It's serious conducting the services, but we have a lot fun otherwise, and that's important, too, as we bond together as brothers."

Rada, who has been a flag-bearer, adds, "I had been on the honor guard at Stillwater for my last three years and then came out to observe at Fort Snelling and started one week later. We have a fantastic group of guys with tons of integrity."

Gary J. Gengler graduated from Anoka High School in 1961 and at age 17 was in basic training five days later at U.S. Navy boot camp in San Diego. He was an E-4 Third Class Petty officer involved in aviation electronics. Gary was aboard the USS *Wasp*, which was a submarine chaser. While based in Rhode Island, they cruised the entire Atlantic and were part of the blockade during the Cuban Missile Crisis in 1962. Most of his civilian career was spent in numerous sales jobs, and he also spent time with Univac. A big history buff, Gengler went back to school at the U of M in Minneapolis to receive his degree in history at the age of 60.

Gengler began his Friday gig in February of 2016 after finding out about the rifle squad at a volunteer recognition dinner for VA volunteers six months earlier. "There were about 1,700 volunteers there, and I sat across from two guys who were members of the rifle squad and they encouraged me to come out. They were on a different day, but there happened to be an opening on Friday. I've always loved guns so I really enjoy being a rifleman. It's an opportunity to shoot in public for a good cause. I just love the coordination of shooting together—it's like live theatre and we are putting on a 10-minute presentation."

"I have been quite surprised at the level of respect the public has for our service with the rifle squad," states the 73-year old New Hope resident. "Whoever I talk to seems to have at least one relative who is buried out here, and almost everybody has been to a funeral here, too. They are really impressed with the honor guard, and that makes me feel good. I really enjoy being on the squad and consider it a great honor."

On a gloomy Memorial Day, the van owned by the Memorial Rifle Squad is parked near the staging area for the annual 10 a.m. festivities at Fort Snelling. I peek in, and facing me is 88-year-old Ted Nemzek, waiting for the service to begin with his daughter and granddaughter. He is very gracious and eager to provide information. I had missed interviewing him on previous visits, but the other fellows had spoken highly of his character and his reverence for the history and tradition of the squad.

When I interview him a few days later at his home in Bloomington, Ted proves to be a fine gentleman. Raised in Moorhead, he enlisted in the Army in 1950 and served until 1953. Two of his brothers were in the military, and one of them fought in Korea at the same time Ted was in combat there and was wounded badly enough to have one of his legs amputated. Ted had attended Moorhead State for two years prior to his service and also had served in the National Guard.

While in Korea, Nemzek earned the rank of Master Sergeant as a forward observer for mortar fire and saw considerable combat overseas. Doing that extremely dangerous job, Ted earned a Bronze Star for his heroics. He spent an additional year with the National Guard following his year in Korea. A member of VFW Post 5555 and Legion Post 435, both in Bloomington, Nemzek sold library books for 20 years with the Society for Visual Education and spent many years working in Chicago. Since joining the Friday squad in 1998, Ted is primarily a rifleman but also served as assistant squad leader for several years.

"It was nice to join an organization where the people think that honoring our deceased veterans is so important," says the inimitable Nemzek. "It is not only honorable to do so but we see it as a necessity. Being a combat veteran, I was well aware of the rifle squad's reputation, and I definitely found a home there. I believe in the concept of doing something for the country and what it stands for."

On a pleasant early June morning, Stephen M. Landgraf proves to be a very engaging interview. Landgraf, who has lived in St. Paul Park for the past 37 years, spends time with the Friday squad only from Memorial Day to Labor Day. The 60-year-old has a good excuse, however. He still works full-time for the city of West St. Paul in street maintenance; he is in his 15th year there and will retire in 2018 and then be out full-time with the rifle squad.

"I was working trimming a tree at work and saw a guy in his yard wearing a Marine Corps cap and it ended up being Jesse Montez, who is on the Friday squad," says a laughing Landgraf. "He told me that I should come out and join them at Fort Snelling. I was still working full-time but then we changed to a four-day (nine-hour) work schedule and I was able to work two hours early on Friday morning and then take two hours of vacation so I could get out here."

Landgraf, who grew up on St. Paul's East Side, is a Marine who joined the rifle squad in 2006 as one of its youngest members. Steve started his four-year active obligation in 1975 and spent most of it in Oahu, Hawaii (Kaneohe Bay), as a Sergeant in the infantry. He also spent time in Australia helping to train military personnel from 14 other nations. He was placed in a Special Services division at one point and even served as a lifeguard in Hawaii for a time, for which he gets constantly teased by his fellow squad members. Landgraf later was in the Marine Reserve for two stints at Fort Snelling before ending his military service in 1983.

"It is the highlight of my life to work with them and a real honor and privilege," says Landgraf about his Friday comrades. "The first five years I was out here, I think hearing 'Taps' made me tear up every time. We have a lot of fun as a group. The banter in the squad room and in the van—it's like being back in boot camp. Yet, when it is time for the services, everybody is serious and the sentiment is heartfelt for the veteran to be buried and their family. While I rotate jobs out here like most everybody else, I prefer being close to the family." Landgraf has also spent the past four years involved in WWII re-enactment activities at schools and community events and even owns an authentic 1942 Jeep and a 1942 Scout car.

Thomas Patrick Mullon, 79, is an upstanding man and one of the most respected members of the rifle squad. A New York native, Tom was raised in Albany and graduated from Christian Brothers Academy in 1955. After earning his history degree from St. Bonaventure in his home state, he enlisted in the U.S. Army in 1961. Tom trained at Fort Dix, New Jersey, and at Fort Sam Houston in Texas, where he received training as a medic. The E-5 Sergeant is a Vietnam veteran, serving aboard aircraft that transported casualties into medical facilities in the Philippines.

Upon discharge from the Army in 1967, Mullon worked as a salesman at Procter & Gamble for a few months. He was encouraged to take the federal exam and quickly was approved to work for the Veterans Administration in Montrose, New York, in 1968. It began a 36-year career working for the VA that would include 15 different jobs in nine states, including two in Minnesota. Mullon jokes, "My wife always said that I could never hold a job."

Tom started out in human resources but then enrolled in graduate school at Columbia University in New York City, where he received a degree in hospital administration in 1971. He moved up to become an assistant hospital director in Montrose before moving to Minnesota in 1984, where he became the director at the VA's Minneapolis hospital. In his 10-year tenure there, he oversaw the construction of the new hospital, which was finished in 1988. He also was the medical district director of five other hospitals in the region.

After retiring in 1994, Mullon then went to work for the state-run Minnesota Veterans Home in Minneapolis as its administrator until 2000. "I was fortunate to be in a position where I could help people get back to life," Tom said about the tie-in between his role as an Army medic and his role as a hospital administrator.

A resident of Eagan for the past 25 years and a member of Legion Post 594 there, Mullon joined the Friday squad in 2000. A good friend of his, former Fort Snelling Cemetery director Bill Napton, encouraged him to join the rifle squad. He had also known George Weiss for years and so he came out on a Friday to observe. "I had been to many funerals out at Fort Snelling over the years and I knew how the squad operated, and I knew that I would be joining at some point," added the classy Mullen.

A rifleman at first, Mullon now serves as one of the day's buglers. In 2003, the Friday squad bugler left and there was no ready replacement. George Weiss asked if anyone had played an instrument, and Tom had played the trombone in high school. He ended up going to Roth Music, and the owner gave him a bugle—and didn't even charge him for it because he knew Tom would be using it for the rifle squad.

"I practiced with the bugle and then started to play at the Friday funerals, but I wasn't very good," says Mullon. "It's actually a lot tougher to play the bugle and it doesn't have the same tone as a trumpet. I switched to a trumpet and got better and now all of our buglers actually play with the trumpet. I also joined the group called 'Buglers Across America,' an organization that helps people learn to play well enough to play at funerals and in public.

After spending his adult life caring for veterans, being on the rifle squad is a natural for Mullon. "It's been an interesting experience, for sure, and we're all here to provide the respect the veteran and their family deserve," adds Tom. "Giving them a send-off only seems proper. It is all about giving honor." Mullon has been a long-time member of the Fort Snelling Volunteer Committee and has served as its president.

Kenneth L. Dallman, who has been an Excelsior resident for 40 years, was born one month after World War II ended in 1945. Ken enlisted in the Navy as an 18-year-old in 1964 and completed eight years in that branch as a machinist's mate. After basic training, Dallman had submarine school in New London, Connecticut, and then nuclear schooling in both California and Idaho. He was then assigned to the USS *Sam Rayburn*, a nuclear submarine that patrolled the Atlantic for six years.

Tom Mullon, one of the Friday buglers, plays the somber 24-note "Taps."

Following active duty, Dallman was employed by Northwestern Bell Telephone for 21 years. During his time at the phone company, he went to night school and earned his degree in business administration. Ken spent five years with the Minneapolis Teachers Retirement Fund before going into real estate development for 15 years. He retired on his 70th birthday.

"I was well aware of the rifle squad's legacy," remarks Dallman. "I always thought I might join it someday, but I started volunteering at the VA hospital as a greeter. I inquired about the rifle squad and was given Mike Pluta's number. He said they didn't have any room at the time, but a few months later there was an opening, and I came out and observed three times and was accepted."

A sharp guy and simply a nice man, the 71-year-old Dallman has been a flag-bearer on the squad since joining in July of 2016. A long-time member of the Legion in Excelsior where he was part of the honor guard, Dallman now is a member with Post 118 in Wayzata. "It's been an honor to serve with the guys on Friday," adds Ken. "We are a tight-knit group, and one of the best things about being out here is that you can be 'real' because we understand each other."

On a beautiful late July summer morning, Ken Gibson is busy assembling the ammunition and flags for the day while George Weiss and Mike Pluta are readying for the squad's arrival. There will be 13 funerals this day, and the mood is somber as it is reported that Ken Dallman was in an accident with his motorcycle in western Minnesota and is recuperating at a Minneapolis hospital. Ken would have major recuperation after having one of his legs amputated below the knee, and his comrades were all ready to assist in helping any way they could.

Amidst concern for others who are suffering with illness, the squad moves on to discuss the addition of a new member and, after a unanimous vote, Joseph P. Ziskovsky becomes the newest member of the Friday squad. The 70-year-old from Shoreview and member of Legion Post 542 Rosetown has observed the past few weeks and is eager to get underway. He learned about the rifle squad a decade ago but happened to meet Pluta at the VA hospital recently. Mike was wearing his Memorial Rifle Squad cap, and Ziskovsky inquired as to what it would take to join. He was told that he could come out and observe and determine if he liked the group and then the squad would determine if they liked him.

"Originally, I found out about them at the state fair one time and I felt like it was something I would do after retiring," says the mild-mannered Ziskovsky. "I also went online to learn more about them. Then, once I met Mike that clinched it for me. I am very appreciative they are having me join."

Ziskovsky was born in San Diego but graduated from high school in Denver (Holy Family) as he traversed the country as a Navy brat, seeing as his father was in the midst of his 20-year career. Joe then received degrees in both biology and physics at Creighton University in 1969. Immediately, Joe enlisted in the Army and served a six-year stint as an E-6 computer operator on Nike missiles. He was stationed in California for more than two years but then, after electronic command school, he worked for the Army Security Agency for more than three years. Joe worked for Texas Instruments as an electrical engineer and worked for PAR Systems in Shoreview and Johnson Screen in New Brighton before retiring.

Chapter 8

Thursday Squad

It is yet another blustery winter morning and the maintenance crew is already busy with their assorted duties. Unfortunately, the wreaths that were placed on the graves are
now gone but it was a pretty sight for the past six weeks. It
is -5 below but this day there is a wind that gusts to 30 miles
per hour. It is bright and sunny, a day for sunglasses. By the
time I arrive at 8:30 a.m., there are already 12 squad members
assembled.

Two separate groups are in the midst of a game of cribbage. After visits to the other four weekday squads, it is apparent that each squad has its own personality and its own
chemistry. Despite their unity in performance while conducting the honor services, each day's squad comports itself a little
differently.

Raymond J. Frisvold, the Thursday squad leader for the
past seven years, eyeballs the hand he has been dealt and wel-
comes me. He is a lighthearted chap who has no concerns for
formality. "Do what you have to do," he tells me, and he's back
to his game. In the squad van later that morning, I find him to
be a real character. Ray, now 85, doesn't go out with the hon-
or guard because of a recent illness. However, he's still present as duty calls. Frisvold joined the fledgling rifle squad the
first week of May in 1979 and became one of the 20 charter

A break in a game of cribbage at the squad room; from left to right:
Harold Braaten, Ray Frisvold, Dave Fleming, Herb Jorgenson, Dave
Mohling, Bill Lee

members in January of 1980. Ray spent his first 12 years on
the Friday squad.

From 1949 to 1979, Frisvold served in the Minnesota National Guard and the 47th Infantry as a receiving clerk. He
was also working as a welder for a whopping 45 years with an
outfit called Moorhead Machinery and Tenten and also Ray-
go Manufacturing. Ray grew up in southwest Minnesota and
graduated from Tracy High School in 1949. He has resided in
Brooklyn Park since 1970 and his 38 years of service in the
rifle squad is surpassed only by founder George Weiss. Jr. His
Legion Post is 630 in Brooklyn Center.

Frisvold was the second youngest of the first volunteers
to the rifle squad in 1979. His first actual honor squad funeral came on September 10, 1979. He recalls, "We had five
guys, besides George, who led the squad. There were four
riflemen—myself, Robert Swanson, Bill Weber, and Anthony
Cuff, and Al Schaeppi was the flag-bearer."

"We just have had good guys out here over the years,"

remarks the understated Frisvold about the current Thursday crew. "These guys are fun to be with, and they are easy to lead."

Interestingly enough, it seems that a heavy majority of the Thursday squad graduated from high school in the early 1960s and are now in their late 60s and 70s. One of them is assistant squad leader Dave Fleming, who has been in that position for the past five years. Dave has lived in St. Paul most of his life but now lives in Centerville. Fleming graduated from Washington High School, which was closed in 1964. A member of the Marine Corps, he spent two tours of duty in Vietnam 1964–68 that involved everything related to transportation.

Fleming, a direct but friendly man, belongs to VFW Post 7555 in Roseville and Legion Post 620 in Hugo. He was a bricklayer for a time but began a career as a St. Paul city fireman in 1983 and retired as a captain after 25 years. He states, "I knew Rick Zech, another fire captain in St. Paul who is on the Tuesday squad, and he convinced me to get involved. I came out on a few Thursdays because that's the day I could fit it in and they let me in. I do whatever Ray Frisvold needs me to do, and I just want to do a good job. These guys are just good people who are dedicated."

In successive visits to the Thursday squad, I found Fleming to be upbeat, observant, and responsible—the kind of guy you'd want by your side in times of trouble or danger. Always assertive, he is a no-nonsense kind of guy who belies his 71 years of age. The others' respect for him is palpable, and he presents a confident aura.

As I head out to interview another Thursday squad member, Fleming grabs my arm and says, "I've got a good one for you, regarding dedication. We had an interested guy out with us one time, and he goes on to tell me that I should call him whenever we need help. I told him that I would never call him because we need to depend on guys every week. We never saw him again."

Frisvold says of Fleming, "Let's face it, I'm pretty much a figurehead now, but Dave is the best man to take over control of the squad. I wouldn't be able to pick anyone better to fill that role. He's the best."

Jim Jore, the historian for the entire rifle squad for the past five years, has his laptop set up in the back room where the rifles and other squad supplies are located. The trim 76-year-old has a dignified presence. The Richfield resident shows me some video he has acquired from the 1930s of the cemetery site and tells me he has hundreds of photos that he assembled for the 35th anniversary celebration of the rifle squad that occurred in 2014. Jore is the perfect guy to keep track of the Memorial Rifle Squad's business, possessing an eye for detail and an affinity for accuracy.

A member of Richfield Post 435, Jore was an Army brat as a youngster, and his father's influence certainly affected his view of the military. Jim served in three different branches over a 24-year period: the Navy Reserves 1964–65 and then active duty 1965–68, the Army National Guard 1976–80 and again 1986–90, and the Army Air Guard 1980–86. Jore specialized in avionics and electronics throughout his military tenure.

After his long stint in the service, Jore spent another 24 years with Control Data in hardware diagnostic engineering. As soon as he retired in 2007, he joined the rifle squad. He states, "My father was buried at Fort Snelling in 2004. Somebody took pictures that day of the honor guard, and I thought that this was something I wanted to do upon retirement. I simply went to the cemetery office to inquire and ended up on the Thursday squad. My week revolves around Thursday—that's how important it is to be out here."

Roger Kohler, who was a welder in the Army's 79th Engineering Battalion, has been on the rifle squad for eight years. Born on Christmas day in 1945, the 71-year-old was one of

The rifle squad readies for a service near the administration building.

the first of the baby-boom generation. He grew up in White Bear Lake and graduated from Hill High School in St. Paul in 1963. He built his own home on Bald Eagle Lake over a 12-year period but now lives in St. Paul. An interesting and pleasant gentleman, Kohler got his welding training at Dunwoody Institute in Minneapolis. Influenced by John Kennedy, he joined the Peace Corps and spent more than two years training welders at a technical school in Ethiopia.

Upon returning from Africa, he was drafted and was in the Army 1968–71. Roger was in the construction battalion stateside, except for one year in Germany. In his civilian career, he continued with welding and was also a manufacturing engineer and a tool-maker. Kohler, who is a member of VFW Post 8752 in Cottage Grove, joined Legion Post 168 in White Bear Lake about 15 years ago and began to learn about the honor guard there. He eventually became the historian for the 4th District Legion. One day, a member of Post 168 was buried at Fort Snelling on a bitterly cold day, and Kohler was hooked.

He came out on a Thursday, met Ray Frisvold, and soon he was active on the squad.

The loquacious Kohler says, "We take no pay, but the gratitude in the families' eyes is so rewarding. Sometimes, a widow is so sad and they are almost inconsolable. But when we bring her the folded flag, she will raise her head and say thank you. I am so proud to be a member of the rifle squad, and I pray that I will see 6,000 volunteer hours as a member, to live long enough to do that. These guys are generous people." So, too, is Kohler, who has been part of the Honor Flight Network since 2005, the group that helps veterans visit the World War II Memorial in Washington, D.C.

James R. Ahlberg is an affable guy and an East Sider from St. Paul. Jim grew up on Arlington Street and graduated from Johnson High in 1966. He has lived in the same house in White Bear Lake for over 40 years. We have to wait for him to finish teasing fellow team-member Bill Lee in order to start our interview. The likeable Ahlberg saw a lot the world, indeed, during his active service in the U.S. Navy 1969–73. Despite being drafted into the Army, he decided to enlist in the Navy and ended up setting foot in 87 countries and six continents. Thus, he was all over both the Atlantic and Pacific Oceans on a destroyer as an E-5 electrician's mate.

A Vietnam veteran, Ahlberg worked as an electrician for Hoist and Derrick as well as Brown and Bigelow for 40 years before retiring in 2003. A member of VFW Post 7555 in Roseville and Legion Post 39 in North St. Paul, Jim joined the Thursday squad in 2009. Now 70, Ahlberg has primarily been a rifleman during his nine years on board.

"I was on a senior bus trip to Branson, Missouri and one of the guys along was on the rifle squad out here," states Ahlberg. "Amazingly, a month later that same guy quit and I was able to replace him. It took a while to adjust back to a military-style uniform again, but I really like them. As for the services, we saw a woman bury her husband in a Quaker-oats cereal box in the urn and a husband bury his wife in a furry beaded purse. The most common urn we have seen, though, is for guys to be buried in 50-caliber ammunition boxes."

Curtis W. Stoltz enlisted in the U.S. Air Force at age 19 after graduating from White Bear Lake High School in 1969. After basic training in Texas, Curt was schooled in Denver, Wichita, and Thailand before heading back to Mississippi for more training. He was an E-5 radar mechanic, a weapons control specialist, and an air traffic control radar technician 1970–79 and served in Duluth, Germany, and Thailand during his stint.

The swarthy Stoltz worked for defense contractors after active service, including McDonnell-Douglas. Within a year of his retirement, he joined the Thursday squad in 2013. Now 66, Curt is a member of VFW Post 9625 in Coon Rapids; he has lived in Andover for over 25 years.

"My father, who was in the Army Air Corps during World War II, was buried out here in 2001," states Stoltz. "I witnessed the honor guard then and knew I wanted to be involved. It's an honor to be able to do this; it's the least we can do for our veterans. I do anything they want me to do on the squad. I am astounded by the variety of containers used for the remains of the deceased and the variety in how families react to the services; some families are all dressed up in suits and dresses and some come in jeans and t-shirts."

Just as we are about to end the interview, Curt mentions that he will be buried at Fort Snelling. As I thank him and shake hands, he said, "My wife, Naida, was buried here in 2011." I tell him I'm sorry to hear that, and he looks downward and says, "Me, too."

James K. (Jim) Johnson was three days from his 71th birthday when interviewed and was one of three rifle squad members having his birthday within the week seated at the same table. After graduating from Wanamingo High School in 1964, Johnson enlisted in the U.S. Army immediately and served for four yours as a personnel management specialist. Most of it was at Fort Richardson in Alaska.

Following service, he spent 23 years each as a steelworker at Paper Calmenson and Contek Machine. He's a member of Legion Post 85 in North Branch, where he is the current Commander, and drives 55 miles one way each Thursday from Rush City to Fort Snelling.

Reserved by nature, Johnson usually carpools with fellow Thursday squad member Carl Anderson, who lives in Harris. Jim joined in 2012. When Clarence Kraemer left the squad a few years later, another bugler was needed. More than 50 years since playing trumpet in high school, Jim took up playing again and now plays with Bob Volk. Inside the squad room after two early funerals, the gentlemanly Johnson says, "I still get emotional over some of the ceremonies, but it is just tremendous to have the opportunity to do this. Sometimes, when I am out in the public and I have my rifle squad cap on, people come up and thank me for my service and it makes you feel so good."

His buddy Carl Anderson has been on the Thursday squad for nine years. He is always one of those firing the rifle volleys and likes it that way. He grew up in Minneapolis and graduated in 1950 from the now-closed Marshall High School. Drafted into the U.S. Army, Corporal Anderson served in Korea for 15 months in reconnaissance. Now a member of VFW Post 6424 in North Branch and Legion Post 139 in Harris, Anderson looks more like a high school wrestler than an 84-year-old retiree.

Carl worked for the U.S. Postal Service for 20 years and also owned his own business. He built clutches for cars and trucks and called himself the "Clutch Doctor." After a friend told him about the rifle squad, he did some checking, and two weeks later he was actively participating on Thursdays. The

Dan Kirchoffner, the squad's chaplain, reads a eulogy for Clara Anderson, wife of Thursday member Carl Anderson, in May of 2017 with members of the Thursday squad in the background.

wiry Anderson tells me about two funerals that really stand out in his time on the squad.

"One time, it was like Mardi Gras out here, and you thought you were in New Orleans," says an amused Anderson. "The people attending the funeral were playing instruments and singing and cavorting about. I've never seen anything like that. On another occasion, the deceased was apparently a big fisherman. His remains were in a fishing box in an urn, and it was in a boat they brought along to the cemetery."

Two days after the 4th of July in 2017, Anderson was speaking in the squad room about another funeral, that of his beloved wife, Clara. Carl had been inactive from the Thursday group for a few months while caring for his spouse. After her death, she was buried on May 11 in Section CC1, Row 15, Site 81A as Anderson shows me the card he carries in his wallet displaying the location of her remains.

"I can't put into words what it meant to have 19 members of the Thursday squad show up in uniform at her funeral," says Anderson. "It means so much to know they were caring for her and for me."

Harold A. Braaten, a 69-year-old Army veteran from Oakdale, hears the conversation and nods in agreement. After a few moments, he says, "I remember one funeral in the summer of 2012. I was standing there as part of the rifle squad, and everybody gets out of their vehicles and they all have on Viking jerseys. We learned later that the deceased was a big fan of both the Vikings and the Twins. The family apparently flipped a coin to see which team jersey they would wear, and they also said that the deceased had season tickets for each team in his hands."

A St. Paul Harding alum from 1966, Braaten was drafted and spent two years in the Army, including one year of combat in Vietnam as a radio operator. Harry earned a Bronze Star for his actions. The easy-going veteran joined the rifle squad in 2010 and mainly serves as a rifleman; he continues to be active with VFW Post 8752 in Cottage Grove and Legion Post 39 in North St. Paul.

Braaten had a 32-year career in education with the Stillwater School District. Harry was an elementary physical education teacher for 17 years and also taught eighth grade health for 15 years. He had a 42-year tenure as a high school swimming official and was president of the local swimming official's association. Braaten also was an assistant and head coach for girls swimming at Tartan and Stillwater Area High Schools.

"Being on the squad has more than met my expectations," adds Harry. "It's an honor to serve alongside these vets. I came out for a funeral for a friend's father in 2011, and I told my wife that I wanted to be a part of it. I came out on a Thursday, and after three visits, I got the okay to get my uniform and I started right away."

Bugler Robert F. Volk, who resides in Plymouth, grew up in Mankato and played in the high school band, graduating in 1949. Bob enlisted in the Air Force right out of school, and the Airman First Class ended up being in an Air Force band for three years, playing the trumpet at parades and military functions. Following active duty, Volk attended the University of Minnesota and received his pharmacy degree. Bob spent a whopping 57 years as a pharmacist and retired at age 80. He even owned two stores—Snyder Westwood Drug in St. Louis Park and Eastside Pharmacy in St. Paul. For 30 years, he played in Big Band–type bands all over the Twin Cities. Bob, who joined the rifle squad in 2007, belongs to Legion Post 435 in Richfield and VFW Post 8752 in Cottage Grove.

On this day, the 86-year-old Volk plays the service song of the branch that the deceased belonged to during their active service. On occasion, he plays a patriotic song while squad members are folding the flag. For many years, he played duets with former squad member Clarence Kraemer, who served 1991–2015 and played on both Tuesdays and Thursdays. Volk, like all the other buglers, actually uses a trumpet, and he has three of them. The one he holds in his hands happens to be one that he purchased as a teenager in 1948 for $220, a tidy sum at that time. I wonder how many notes have been played on that 67-year-old instrument.

A truly genuine man, Volk is a just a sweet guy, and nobody on the squad gives him a hard time. Still, he relishes all the tomfoolery. "It's just been a great experience to be on the rifle squad," states a beaming Volk. "The personnel we have are unmatched, and you can't beat the chemistry we have together. In the end, it is wonderful to have the sense of giving back and honoring our vets who served."

On a picturesque winter day in late February, there are 18 squad members present when Pierre "Pete" Nadeau drops by for a visit. Nadeau served on Thursdays 2000–13 and he is greeted with open arms. It's a scene that I witnessed many times, seeing the slaps on the back and hearing the barbs, supposed insults, and backhanded compliments (translation: a way for a man to show affection to another man). I'm told he was in the Korean conflict and that he saw heavy action at the Chosin Reservoir in late 1950. Those within earshot nod their heads in tribute to his service, be it active duty or with the honor squad.

Daniel D. Kirchoffner serves as the chaplain for the Memorial Rifle Squad, a fitting position for a man who is a permanent deacon at St. Genevieve Catholic Church in Centerville. In his 30 years as a deacon, Dan has also served at St. John the Baptist in Hugo and at Transfiguration in Oakdale. Kirchoffner also serves as the chaplain for Legion Post 620 in Hugo, where he lives.

A quiet and unassuming person, the 76-year-old Kirchoffner joined the Thursday squad in 2012 and normally serves as a rifleman. Dan grew up in Devil's Lake, North Dakota, enlisted in the U.S. Navy, and served 1959–62. As an E-3 electronics technician, he cruised throughout the Pacific but was based at the Naval Air Station in Hawaii. The person responsible for him joining the rifle squad was Nadeau.

"I really like the people we have out here," says Kirchoffner, who was a corporate safety engineer and had a 31-year career at 3M. "We are a family and we take care of each other. No doubt, we are quite a diverse group, but we have a common goal in the end: to give honor and respect for the deceased who gave to their country."

Robert C. (Joe) Johansen is one of the few squad members who was on active duty in the U.S. Coast Guard. Joe was raised in South Dakota and served in the Coast Guard 1965–69. He spent more than two years overseas as an E-4 boatswain, traversing the South Pacific. Following his active duty, Johansen got his degree from the University of Minnesota in food science. After several years in the food industry, Joe made a career change and built energy plants, even becoming a vice president and general manager for Koda Energy.

Johansen, now 69, volunteers at the Veterans Affairs Medical Center on Wednesdays, escorting or greeting visitors. A resident of Lakeville after living in Burnsville for nearly 30 years, Johansen is generally a flag-bearer on Thursdays. Joe belongs to Legion Post 1776 in Apple Valley and joined the rifle squad in 2012. "One of my friends talked to me about it and I was impressed with what they were doing," remarks Johansen. "I was put on a list for six months and was pleased to be accepted."

"I enjoy seeing the dynamics of the family during the ceremony," says Johansen. "We see a wide range in regard to the size of the assemblage for the service and also in their reaction to it. There is a real gamut of emotions—from complete grief and sadness to stoic acceptance of the deceased passing. Once, the wife of the deceased was to receive the flag for the husband. There was a young woman, who was in full military uniform, who we found out was the daughter. She was on bended knee and presented the flag to her mother. Wow, there wasn't a dry eye for anyone who witnessed that."

Donald L. Patrick, a 79-year-old resident of Bloomington, is a sharp, progressive guy with a clever wit. Like almost any other member who was in the Marines, he makes sure I know that he is still a Marine. He was in the Corps 1960–66 after growing up in St. Louis Park and graduating from high school there in 1956. He finished with the rank of corporal. After training at Parris Island and Camp Lejeune, Don was in the FMF 26th Rifle Company Reserve unit at Wold International in the Twin Cities.

A member of Legion Post 435 in Richfield, Patrick lived for 42 years in Edina while he was laboring in the toy industry. Don was in quality management for different companies and spent nine years traveling all over the world. Patrick joined the Thursday group in 2008 and usually has the role of rifleman. He is also involved with Camp Hastings, a military museum in Hastings, where he has been involved for over 30 years. In fact, they have built two World War II quonset huts at their Hastings site. He has also participated with a Marine Corps living history group for decades in the Twin Cities.

"Jim Jore told a buddy of mine about the squad, and we came out and observed and really liked it," states Patrick about his entrance onto the Thursday contingent. "We have a good bunch of guys, and the best thing about them is that they tolerate me."

Mark T. Knapp was born in Portland, Oregon, and graduated from high school in Salem, but he has lived in Eagan for over 30 years. He joined the U.S. Army in 1971 and was on active duty for two years, most of it at Fort Lee, Virginia, as a military policeman, cook, and guard. However, he joined the Army Reserve in Scottsdale, Arizona, upon fulfilling his stint in 1973. With 24 years in the Reserve, he ended his military career of 27 years in 1997.

He has been on the rifle squad since 2014 after retiring from a career in the airline industry. Knapp, a quiet and reserved type, was a safety instructor and then an inspector for Northwest Airlines 1981–2006. Mark is generally a flag-bearer when out at Fort Snelling and is an active member at Legion Post 1776 in Apple Valley.

"I explored other volunteer opportunities after retirement but this one fit me," says the 66-year old Knapp. "I would drive through every once in a while, and thought it would be interesting. It has been impressive to listen to all the World War II and Korean War vets," says Knapp. "I've learned a lot about history from those guys."

On an early April morning under a cloudy sky, there are to be funeral ceremonies for 14 and most of them will be held at the columbarium. In the past decade, more than 70% of the ceremonies have been conducted there as traditional casket burials have become much less common. The members are dressed warmly, but no one is really complaining as the winds started to gust to 35–40 miles an hour.

In the van waiting for the first funeral is Herbert E. Jorgensen, a spry 88-year-old with a friendly, mild-mannered demeanor that befits his role as a presenter to the families. Herb was first in the Air Force (16 years) but then in the Army (4 years) from late 1948 to early 1969. He knows his service dates by heart, which is not a surprising development for these fellows.

Jorgensen graduated from Montevideo High School in 1947. In the Air Force, he was a Technical Sergeant and was a personnel worker on a bomb squadron while in Korea and was in country when the armistice was signed in July 1953. He also was an investigator for that branch. In the Army, Herb was a Warrant Officer. In civilian life, the current Apple Valley resident worked in court security at the federal courthouse in St. Paul and also was an Internal Revenue Service investigator for 15 years. Herb, who belongs to Legion Post 1776 in Apple Valley, joined the Thursday squad in 2003 and served for a time as the assistant squad leader.

Queried about his experience on the squad, Herb says, "It's been fantastic because we have such a good group of guys here; we get along well, and coming here is the highlight of the week for me. I feel that the job is very rewarding for me. I have some very good friends here, for sure, but a guy better not have a thin skin to be out here."

Just back from his winter residence in Florida is David F. Mohling, who has served since 2005. Dave grew up on a farm in northeast Iowa, graduated from high school in 1960, and was drafted into the U.S. Army in 1964. He was a Spec. 4 company clerk during his two-year stint, serving a year in Vietnam.

The 75-year-old Mohling then spent an impressive 43 years with North Central, Republic, and Northwest Airlines. Dave was in customer service, and his calm and reassuring manner would be appropriate for his job demands; he worked in Oshkosh, Wisconsin, Chicago, and Orlando before coming to Minneapolis for his final 20 years. A resident of New Market/Elko since 2003, he is a member at Legion Post 586 in nearby Lonsdale. Like most members, he alternates positions on Thursday as a rifleman, flag-bearer, or presenter.

"Because I worked at the airport, I was across the street

The Thursday squad gathers for a group photo in the summer of 2017.

from Fort Snelling and had witnessed the rifle squad on many occasions," states Mohling. "I wanted to give back, and this made sense for me; it is my favorite day of the week coming out here. The families are always so appreciative, and it makes the time all very worthwhile."

Howard A. Kittleson is full of appreciation for a lot of things. One is for still being able to do things like volunteer for the Memorial Rifle Squad, which he has done since 2005. In 2012, he wasn't expected to live after having brain surgery and spent three months in the hospital. He lost 20% of his brain function in that operation and is blind in the right eye. Howard can't drive, either, but he's out with the Thursday squad every week, yet another example of the dedication of the rifle squads.

The engaging and talkative Howard grew up in Turtle Lake, Wisconsin, but has resided in Newport for nearly 45 years. Now 78, Howard was in the Marine Corps for seven years (1956–63) and was an E-5 Sergeant. Kittleson was a forward observer for the artillery in Vietnam. On his fourth day in country, Howard was wounded in the right ankle, right knee, right elbow, and back. It was the first time that he was a shot at, too. He spent six months in hospitals in Japan, Hawaii, and California. After release from the military, he worked for many years for Dahlen Transport.

A member of Legion Post 98 in St. Paul Park and VFW 8752 in Cottage Grove, Kittleson carries the chrome rifle during the honor ceremonies. He served as an assistant squad leader for Thursdays for six years and relishes his time out at Fort Snelling. "I really love doing the job we do out here," says a sincere Kittleson, who is proud to say that he built his own house. "The reason why I came out for Thursday is that my wife's dad had his funeral out here on that day. My wife and her two sisters said then that I needed to come out here and work with these guys; I was lucky that I only needed to wait one day to get in."

Gregory A. Munson moved to Rosemount a few years ago and is now saving on gas transporting himself back and forth to Fort Snelling National Cemetery. The U.S. Army veteran (1966-68) joined the Thursday squad in 2013, and for two years he drove 110 miles one-way from Webster, Wisconsin, to volunteer. In fact, in 2014 he drove a total of 11,123 miles to do his service. He shrugs his shoulders and says, "It's what I had to do to get here."

A St. Paul native and a graduate of Central High in 1964, Munson was drafted and served in the infantry for two years. Greg was in the 8th Army Honor Guard after training at Fort Leonard Wood, Missouri, and Fort Lewis, Washington. He was in the United Nations command in Seoul, South Korea, for 13 months, providing security for generals, colonels, and majors and other visiting dignitaries. Greg worked with a team of 16 for the command center. In civilian life thereafter, he worked for 28 years as a fireman for the city of St. Paul, ultimately reaching the rank of captain.

Now 70, the classy Munson is a member of Legion Post 47 in Hastings and is happy to play whatever role he can on

Thursday's squad. He adds, "I mostly carry the flags or shoot the rifle but I am glad to go wherever they put me. I was in charge of the honor guard for the fire department, so I knew the general procedures of what we do well. Two of the guys on our squad there came out here, Dave Fleming and Bill Lee, and it was always part of my plan to join them out here. Our leaders, Ray and Dave, have a lot of common sense, and it is just enjoyable to be a part of it all."

William D. Lee is one of Munson's colleagues with the St. Paul Fire Department along with Fleming and is busy playing cribbage when I interview him back at the squad room. Bill worked as a fireman for 27 years at four different stations and also retired as a captain. The youngest man (61) on the Thursday squad, the upbeat Lee came on the Thursday squad in 2009. He grew up in West St. Paul and graduated from Henry Sibley in 1974. He has lived in adjacent South St. Paul for nearly 40 years and he jokes that he is still considered an outsider.

Following high school, Bill enlisted in the U.S. Navy and served for three years cruising the Pacific Ocean aboard the USS *Midway* as an aircraft handler on the flight deck. A member at Legion Post 98 in St. Paul Park and VFW Post 5 in North St. Paul, Lee rotates his roles on the squad but enjoys being a presenter. Like Greg Munson, he also served on the honor guard with the St. Paul Fire Department and was familiar with the general routine of conducting such ceremonies. He came at the same time as Fleming. The easy-going Lee is obviously comfortable with his group and says, "Our squad leader, Ray, is a fun guy, and we all get along. I plan on being out here a long time, and like most of the other guys, I plan to be buried out here when I'm gone."

On a beautiful spring day with the trees finally in full bloom, the cemetery glistens like an emerald jewel. Upon greeting the six gentlemen assembled in the squad room two hours before the first service, I have a chance to interview Donald J. Fineran.

Don drives from East Bethel every Thursday, where he has lived for almost 40 years. He is a personable guy and effusive in his responses to questioning.

A Hooiser from Indiana, Fineran enlisted in the U.S. Army at age 21 in 1968 and served for four years. After training at Fort Dix and Fort Benning, Don went to Fort Rucker, Alabama, for helicopter instruction. In Vietnam just a month, Fineran was in a helicopter crash and suffered lower leg injuries; he spent six months recuperating at a hospital stateside and was given a medical discharge.

Don was in education for 41 years, 35 of them spent as a guidance counselor at Spring Lake Park High School. He also coached boys' and girls' track and field and cross-country. Fineran got his physical education degree from Indiana State and his degree in guidance counseling and psychology from Northern Colorado.

Fineran, now 70, belongs to VFW Post 6316 in Blaine. He joined the squad immediately after retirement in 2015 and generally is a flag-bearer. The thoughtful former educator reflects, "I've always had a lot of guilt for not completing my tour and being out here is my way of doing that. I was on the color guard at Fort Benning, so I was aware of what these groups do, and then I saw a television bit on the Fort Snelling guys and knew I would join as soon as I could."

"Doing the funerals can be very repetitive with us doing one every 15 minutes and can seem boring at times, but then you realize that it's the only service for that family," remarks Fineran, who also volunteers at the Veteran Affairs Medical Center on Mondays. "Some people come up and thank us and it means a lot."

Sitting next to Fineran is 68-year-old David G. Schwalbe, who became a part of the Thursday crew in the summer of 2016. Schwalbe also drives a good distance from Cologne to volunteer—37 miles. A humble and genial man, David doesn't

The Thursday rifle squad set to fire their customary three-volley rounds.

join in on the hijinks, but he relishes the camaraderie of the group and states, "I just enjoy working with the guys and I get treated well even when they are just goofing around. It's so interesting to talk to everybody and learn about their military experience and what their life is like now."

Schwalbe was raised in Chaska and graduated from that city's high school in 1966. David was inducted into the U.S. Army in 1968 and trained at Fort Leonard Wood before a one-year tour in Vietnam. He worked as a Spec. 4 engineer and helped to purify water at a treatment plant while overseas. Following active service in 1970, Schwalbe then worked an astounding 45 years for the Menasha Corporation in Lakeville.

A member of Legion Post 57 in Chaska where he lived for most of his adult life, David has mostly been a flag-bearer in his first months with the squad but has also been a rifleman. "I always used to come out for Memorial Day services," states Schwalbe. "I watched the rifle squad and thought I would like to do that upon retirement. Both my wife and I have relatives buried at Fort Snelling."

Then Schwalbe tells me that his wife, Veronica, died in 2015 and was buried here, appropriately enough on a Thursday. Less than a year later, David was on the Thursday squad. I express my condolences, and we have a quiet moment together. There is no need for any more inquiries. It takes me a few moments to compose myself as we shake hands.

David E. Davidson grew up in a small town in southern Minnesota called Emmons, which is still his permanent residence. Emmons is 120 miles from Fort Snelling, and yet Davidson has driven that distance once a week for three years to do his service with the Thursday group. Unfortunately, he has recently required radiation treatments for prostate cancer and has to be temporarily housed at the VA grounds in order to get his medical care.

David was drafted into the U.S. Army in 1965 and served for two years as a Private in the transportation sector, mainly unloading bombs and explosives. David was in Vietnam for 10 months and was discharged from active duty in 1968. The unassuming Davidson was a welder for many years with American Hoist in St. Paul.

A member of VFW Post 1350 in North St. Paul and Legion Post 404 in Alden, Minnesota, the 72-year-old Davidson usually carries the chrome rifle during the honor guard ceremonies. He heard about the rifle squads through the grapevine and decided to come out on a Thursday to observe. Davidson tells me, "I visited and met the qualifications so I joined up. It's quite an honor and privilege to salute the deceased and give them their last farewell to our comrades in arms."

Wayne G. Bauer has lived in Hastings all his life. He grew up on a farm near the city and graduated from Hastings High in 1967. Enlisting in the Marine Corps at age 17, Bauer was inducted into the military at Met Stadium as part of the famous

"Twins Platoon" where 150 soldiers started their service career. Wayne served a four-year stint and was awarded a Purple Heart after being wounded not long after the Tet offensive in 1968. He was given the medal in May of that year but went back into combat after his wounds healed.

Bauer became a Thursday squad member in 2013 after retiring from Con Agra Foods in 2011, where he worked for 40 years. He brings fellow squad member Howard Kittleson to Fort Snelling each week after sharing breakfast together on Howard's dime. The straightforward Marine belongs to VFW Post 1210 in Hastings, and he is on the honor guard there, as well. He also is a member of Legion Post 47 in Hastings. Normally a rifleman at Fort Snelling, Bauer was encouraged to join by a Hastings friend, Ed Mays, who served on Mondays.

"I am surprised with how many funerals we do sometimes," says the soft-spoken Bauer, who recently turned 68. "We are usually jam-packed with funerals, but that's why we're here, to give each family a nice send-off."

Chapter 9

Wednesday Squad

On the first of my visits on a late January morning, it is a light day for funerals, with just six former military personnel to be buried with full honors. There are 19 rifle squad members assembled, led by little Leo Noe, the Wednesday squad leader. The 85-year-old St. Paul resident has been on the squad since 1994. The slight fellow is obviously likeable. After pleasantries are exchanged, he tells me that he might have to head home early today to care for his wife, who has been ill.

Leo Noe served in the U.S. Navy 1950-54 after growing up on a farm near Little Falls and graduating from St. Paul Washington High School. Noe was aboard the USS *Island*, which carried seaplanes, during the Korean War. Leo was a 1st Class Machinist-mate during his four-year stint and was a mechanical engineer in civilian life. He has been the Wednesday squad leader for 15 of his 21 years volunteering with the rifle squad. A member of Legion Post 542 in Roseville, Leo says he joined when he found out friends of his from the post belonged.

"A vast majority of the guys on this squad are extremely dedicated," Noe says. "The camaraderie among the group is the main reason I am here and, of course, to honor our deceased vets, too. Since I have been with this day's volunteers, we have had 23 guys who shared duties with us die themselves. So, even though they may be buried out here on another day, our whole

MEMORIAL RIFLE SQUAD VOLUNTEERS

The Wednesday squad is pictured in front of their 2014 Ford van during the summer of 2017.

Wednesday squad will be there with them on whatever day they are buried. A lot of guys from the other days show support when one of the rifle squad members dies and they line up as a courtesy patrol."

James M. (Jim) Anderson, a first-class gentleman, offers to make me at home with the squad and is quick to answer my general queries about the squad. He was raised in St. Paul and graduated from St. Paul Central in 1966. He enlisted in the Air Force after high school and served four years as a jet aircraft mechanic, mostly at Travis Air Force base in California. As a civilian, he spent a long career with Deluxe Corporation as a pressman. Now a member of Rosetown Legion Post 542, Anderson has spent five years on the Wednesday squad rotating positions within the group.

"Leo Noe recruited me from our post and I felt it was an honor to be asked," says Anderson, who was Commander at Rosetown for three years and is now the American Legion District 4 Vice Commander. "The experience has been even better than I expected. You feel sad at some of the funerals where there is hardly anyone there; it just tears me apart that the deceased veteran is all alone. But it gives me comfort that we are there for them."

A member since 2010, Anderson is eager to tell me about his experience venturing out to Washington, D.C., for Memorial Day services at Arlington National Cemetery in 2014 when the Fort Snelling squad was honored for their 35 years of service. Jim says, "There were 11 of us from the rifle squad on the trip, and Sun Country Airlines moved us from coach to first class when they heard we were with the rifle squad. I was so impressed by that gesture, and I tell everybody how sold I am on them as a company. A flag was specifically made for us for that special event, and I had the honor of carrying that flag for the rifle squad. I was just in awe that I was able to represent our group and to be a part of it."

Howard Tellin, the bugler for Wednesdays, is a fountain of knowledge about the rifle squads. A spry 75-year-old, Tellin looks fit enough to play middle linebacker for the Vikings. Currently a resident of Cottage Grove, Howard has been a member of the rifle squad since 1996. In fact, for the first three years, he volunteered on both Tuesdays and Thursdays. After graduating from Cass Lake High School in northern Minnesota in 1960, he spent six years in the U.S. Army. He was in Vietnam for three years in the Mekong Delta with the 9th Infantry and spent the other three with the 101st Airborne Reconnaissance.

An active member of VFW Post 8752 in Cottage Grove, Legion Post 98 in St. Paul Park, and Vietnam Veterans of America 470 in Anoka, Tellin has been the bugler for the Wednesday squad since 1999. He also spends considerable time maintaining the pre–World War I rifles used by all the squads. I am informed that there are 60 rifles in total but only 40 are used regularly and just eight, at maximum, each day. The rifles are Springfield 1903 and Springfield 1903-A3 models. All the parts are interchangeable so it makes for a good situation for cleaning and maintenance. The guns are identical except for the sights and the magazine, which doesn't matter, of course, because the riflemen use blanks.

The former Army Sergeant takes care of rifles for the entire squad, and it is a task he relishes, just like his role as the bugler. To the novice, the bugle he is holding this day could have been five years old. No, it's 62 years old, purchased by Tellin in 1955. Howard saunters out for the funeral of a former Navy man and his 24-note playing of "Taps" is sharp and in rhythm. Upon returning to the van, an observer says, "Still got it," Tellin retorts," I'm not sure I ever had it, but these brass horns just don't like cold weather. "

"I could have been on the original squad out here at Fort Snelling in 1979," adds Tellin. "But I blew it off because we couldn't even get enough guys for an honor guard at our own post. Back in 1970, I played at a ceremony out here when Denny Christy called me for Post 1296 in Bloomington and then I did one a year later, too. It's been great to be doing this, and we are certainly a team."

For the first funeral of the day, Patriot Guard Minnesota showed up to pay their respects. Founded in 2006, this all-volunteer group helps ensure honor, dignity, and respect for the deceased by standing at attention with the American flag at memorial services. They attend funerals only at the invitation of the fallen's immediate family or their representative, such as a funeral director. It is 30 degrees but a strong breeze from the north makes it feel much colder. Some came by car or truck but several came with their customary motorcycles. By the time the family and friends of the deceased arrive, more than two dozen of the Patriots are present.

I ask John Burkhard, a lighthearted chap from Falcon Heights, was asked why he joined the rifle squad, and he replies, "Leo Noe and Dutch Harlan recruited me at gunpoint!" After the laughter subsides, he adds, "I came on the scene when I retired after 42 years of working for the Northern Pacific and Burlington

Northern Railroads as a conductor." Now 70, Burkhard has been on the squad since 2007. He served in both Germany and Greece 1966–68 in the Army as a mortar specialist, working alongside NATO forces.

John belongs to both Rosetown Post 7555 and Legion Post 620 out of Hugo. A man of few words, he makes a succinct com-

The Patriot Guard

ment after someone mentions that Wednesdays are usually pretty light days for funerals. He matter-of-factly says, "Light days means we don't have to bury as many guys, and that's good."

Robert H. Nelson of Apple Valley is a fun-loving 71-year-old who enjoys poking the needle in his fellow squad members. In the midst of his Rodney Dangerfield–like insults, it is also clear that this is a guy who treasures his role on the squad. But he also gets the "big picture" of why they are out here on these cold winter days. "My wife knows that she has to work around doing anything on Wednesday with me because of my participating with these guys. We are here to honor veterans, and the really cool thing is that it doesn't matter what branch they served in, their rank, or anything about their service—it's that everybody is the same and they get the same treatment."

An Army combat engineer and construction mechanic 1963–66, Bob has been on the Wednesday squad for nine years after a long career in the tape department at 3M. He also spent time in construction and driving bus and working as a custodian for the Richfield School District. Bob is active with Legion Post 1776 in Apple Valley, where he says the fish dinners are fantastic. He was the Commander at Apple Valley and was the overall rifle squad Commander in 2011. Proud that he is one of 11 members from Post 1776 with the Fort Snelling Memorial Rifle Squad, Bob Nelson has also been on six honor flights bringing WWII veterans to Washington, D.C.

A true character, Nelson is the epitome of a rifle squad member—he's a barrel of laughs in the squad room and on the bus, but he's all business when the honor guard is performing. He makes sure to highlight how important the honor flights are for those WWII vets. He remarks, "One guy didn't talk on the entire flight out to D.C., but on the way home he was effusive in giving the volunteers a thank you for bringing him to the World War II Memorial. He also talked almost nonstop about being on the Bataan death march. His son, who accompanied him on his honor flight, told me he had never heard him speak a word about it."

Michael D. Hanzal grew up in the West 7th area of St. Paul and attended Archbishop Brady High School in West St. Paul, a Catholic school that now houses St. Croix Lutheran. Now 67, Mike was drafted into the U.S. Army after graduation in 1968 and served in Vietnam as an infantryman with the 25th Infantry. Mike was wounded at 19 and earned a Bronze Star for his bravery in action. Besides his Purple Heart, he still has the shrapnel wounds to prove it and ever-present heart problems to boot.

"I received my Bronze Star on September 11, so 9-11 has a double meaning for me," says Hanzal. "You are proud of getting your medal but it also brings sadness for all you experienced and witnessed. Plus, the terrorist attack in New York is also a reminder of tough times."

Mike joined the rifle squad in 2011, following his friends John Sobaski and Bernie Bondurant. Hanzal states, "I was friends with those guys and so it was natural for me to come out on Wednesdays. I am very comfortable with the squad because there are a lot of Vietnam vets on it, and we get along very well and can identify with each other. I definitely plan on being out here 20–25 years."

"They call me the social director," says the gregarious Hanzal. "I help to organize root-beer floats in the summer and fish fries, too, and then we have a bratwurst party in October. Everybody comes and they contribute and have a good time." Mike gets along with everybody and is a sought-after personality.

Like most guys who serve, Hanzal freely moves from one job to the other with the rifle squad. He has been coming on Wednesdays for six years after retiring from a career as a floor coverer, mostly carpet and tile. For the final 15 years, the North St. Paul resident and member of VFW Post 295 in South St. Paul owned his own company. On successive visits on Wednesdays, Hanzal always has a ready smile and a good word for all he encounters.

Mike relates one final story. His father, a WWII Marine veteran who fought at Iwo Jima, died early in 2011 and was buried at Fort Snelling. On the one-year anniversary of his death on January 11, Hanzal grabbed the Marine Corps flag that day for the day's services. He remembers, "All of a sudden, a gust of wind came up and the flag hit me on the side of the head and on my cheek. I know that was my dad." For most of the past year, Hanzal has served as an assistant squad leader, taking over more of the responsibilities for Leo Noe.

Clarence L. Dick is a reserved and respectful man who belies his age of 83. An East-Sider from St. Paul to this day, Clarence graduated from Johnson High. While he doesn't partake in the banter, you can tell he enjoys it by his wide smile when the others berate each other's service branch. Dick served in the U.S. Navy 1952–56 where he was a machinist's mate. He belongs to VFW Post 7555 in Roseville and Legion Post 577 at Arcade-Phalen in

**Mike Hanzal (second from left) and Clarence Dick (second from right)
are at attention at an honor service, joined by two active members of
the Department of Defense.**

his old neighborhood. His service at Fort Snelling dates back to
1998, and he has always been on the Wednesday squad; in civilian life, he spent most of his time as a factory worker at 3M. He
was overall Squad Commander in 2007.

"The Wednesday group is a boisterous bunch," the straight-
faced Dick adds. "We all have fun but we know why we are
here, and everybody is always professional when we conduct
our ceremonies. I have always been aware of this existence of
this organization and wanted to join as soon as I retired."

One of those boisterous fellows is Gordon L. Carlson. Soon
to be 93, Carlson is a character in every sense of the word. Another East-Sider from St. Paul, Carlson chortles after telling
me that he has a lot of kids all over St. Paul. The other guys
giggle while he tells me, with a wink, that he delivered milk
in the city for 37 years. Gordy howls as loud as all the others
combined. After the jokes die down, I verify that he did, indeed,

spend those 37 years as a milkman working for Sanitary Farm Dairies, which was later bought out by Land O'Lakes. I later found out he has been married to a gal named Delores for a whopping 67 years.

These fellows may carry on some, but they are not the type to pad their resumes or brag about their accomplishments. Somebody says that I should ask about Carlson's work at the VA Hospital. I tell Gordy that my wife just retired from there after 30 years as a pharmacist. Well, he notifies me that he spent 60—yes, 60—years volunteering as the hospital chairman for the VFW, setting up activities for the veterans. That means he started that task in 1954. One of his comrades nudges me to tell me that he was the overall Commander of the rifle squads in 2008. Jim Hogan whispers, "We consider Gordy our mascot; we love having him out here."

Carlson graduated from Johnson High in 1943 and entered the U.S. Navy that year. He was discharged in 1946, the same years as my father. When I told him so, he said that they probably shared a beer somewhere in the Pacific. Gordy was a storekeeper and ran two warehouses in the supply department. Carlson was mainly in the South Pacific during WWII and was even on Guadalcanal after it was secured.

A member of VFW Post 7775 in Roseville, Carlson found out from some of the members there that the rifle squad was short a few guys back in 1984. "I came out on a Wednesday, and I have been with these guys for the past 33 years," said the gregarious Carlson, who lives in Oakdale. "You couldn't find a better bunch of fellows, they are so helpful to all the other members and they are just terrific. Whenever one of our members dies, from any of the day's squads, it is so great to see the members from the other days' squads come to the funeral to pay their respects."

During my visit to that day's squad room, Richard D. Asbury proves to be one of the most helpful members of the Wednesday squad and one of the first to arrive to prepare for the services. Rich was born in Superior, Wisconsin, but graduated from Duluth East in 1963. The following year he joined the U.S. Army and was discharged five years later. Asbury reached the rank of Sergeant E-5 and was a combat engineer. Rich served for 12 months in Vietnam and 13 months in South Korea.

Now 70 and a 25-year resident of Blaine, Asbury belongs to VFW 6316 in that northern suburb. A machinist for 30 years following active duty, Rick retired from that career in 1997.

The rifle squad lines up as a family gathers to honor the deceased.

However, he actually started on the Wednesday squad in 1994 and is now in his 23rd year with the group. A man without pretense, Asbury has nothing but praise for the rifle squad, for which he has served as the quartermaster for the overall group for the past 15 years.

"We have the standard items that we issue to new members of the squads, but we try to give them whatever they need," remarks Asbury. "As long as it is reasonable and keeps us looking professional, we want them to be comfortable. During a miserable winter a few years ago, we got the guys hand-warmers and hoodies, for example. I get a lot of help from Gary Klein, Jim Hogan, and Al Spangenberg, who come in early to help with our supplies."

"I first heard about the rifle squads when I saw a television clip on it years ago," says Asbury, who is usually a flag-bearer but also has been a presenter. "I came out the next week, in fact, and there was no wait to get in. I am so proud of what we do here. We are just repaying a lot of these people for their service to the country; they would do it for us if they could, I'm certain. I am so glad I will be buried out here someday."

As I shake hands and am about to move on to another interview, Rich blurts out, "You know, we got the best squad out here." It is a refrain I hear from every squad, and none of them are wrong.

George E. Fischer comes off as a very bright man on a first observation. It turns out to be accurate. He was bright enough to get through dental school at the University of Minnesota and was a periodontist in Edina for many years. The slender Fischer also taught at the U of M one day a week for 28 years. Looking much younger than his 82 years, George looks fit as a fiddle while lined up as a rifleman.

Now a resident of Bloomington after many years of living in Edina, Fischer joined the Wednesday squad in 2002 and is still an active member of Legion Post 533 in Hopkins. George joined the U.S. Air Force in 1960 after graduating from the Catholic high school in Marshall, Minnesota, and finishing dental school. He was a dentist in the military and became a captain, eventually working at Canadian radar sites and becoming Commander of a dental unit at Fort Stewart Air Force base in Newburgh, New York.

What prompted the unassuming Fischer to join the rifle squad? "I had seen the video from WCCO television on the Friday squad and it intrigued me, but then 9-11 happened and that did it for me. I came out and observed on a Wednesday and was accepted, and I have been here for the past 15 years. You can't beat being with a great bunch of guys."

As I finish my interview with Fischer, Jim Hogan says, "He's too modest to tell you about his model railroad set and all the work he does for the Hill House, so ask him about it." Sure enough, Fischer belongs to the Great Railway Society and apparently has a phenomenal model set at his home. George tells me that he has a big interest in the James J. Hill House on Summit Avenue in St. Paul and that he is a major philanthropist there.

James W. Hogan is one of those guys who seems to know a lot about a lot of things. Above all, he is a people supporter and is the likely one to inform me about somebody else's plaudits, be they service-connected or not. Jim is a nimble 78-year-old with quick retorts to all my inquiries. He's eager to tell me he has loads of photos of the Wednesday squad if there is a need for them and that historian Jim Jore of the Thursday squad has photos of each day's squad from the 35th anniversary book on the rifle squad compiled in 2014.

An Eagan resident since 1970, Hogan joined the Wednesday crew 13 years ago after a long career with the state of Minnesota working in economic security with managed computer operations. Jim had grown up in Richfield and graduated from Minneapolis DeLaSalle High School in 1957. Soon after, he enlisted in the U.S. Air Force and served 1958–61. Hogan was an Airman First Class and was in the Security Service. For three years, Jim was stationed at an Army base just south of Frankfurt, Germany. He worked for 12 straight days and then had four days off to travel around Europe on a 1949 BMW motorcycle he purchased there.

"It was quite an experience to see Europe with four days off and, of course, you could get to a lot of places from there in that time," says Hogan. "I even brought the BMW home but sold it later. For a young guy, it was a real special to see so much and learn about those countries and their cultures."

Hogan's brother-in-law, Mike Ivers, was on the Wednesday squad, and so Jim decided to join him in 2004. Jim had joined AmVets 1 in Mendota in order to be eligible to be accepted on the squad. Unfortunately, Ivers died in 2005. "I would never leave the Wednesday squad because I love these guys," states Hogan. "Gosh, they are a bunch of characters and they make me laugh, but they buckle down when it comes time for the funeral and service."

"Perhaps the most memorable story I can relate about the rifle squad came one day when we were preparing for the day in the squad room," adds Hogan, who has a memory like a computer. "Two gals, who were probably in their 40's, come to us and ask if we could do something for their father, who was buried at Fort Snelling before the rifle squad started here in 1979. So, we had a service for their dad before our customary funerals started, and that really made their day."

There are two guys named "Al" on the Wednesday squad. One is "Little Al" and the other, not surprisingly, is "Big Al." Alton S. Lilja is "Little Al" and he is... little, perhaps 5' 3" and 150 pounds; he tells me on a later occasion that he used to be 5'5". Alton didn't join the rifle squad until he was 74 years old, one of the oldest to ever join a squad. Now 85, he's still out here after 11 years of service and intends to continue to do so, even though he is becoming a bit frail. At the services, "Little Al" always carries one of the flags and it's usually the U.S. Army flag.

Alton Lilja joined the U.S. Army in 1954 after growing up in Randall, Minnesota, and graduating from Little Falls High in 1950. Lilja was in the service for three years and was an E-5 helicopter mechanic during that tenure and was stationed in Germany for 29 months. Following his discharge in 1957, he was an airline mechanic and then an inspector for many years with North Central, Republic, and then Northwest Airlines for a whopping 42 years. The quiet and laid-back "Little Al" has been a 27-year member of Legion Post 1776 in Apple Valley and also is a member of VFW Post 9433 in nearby Rosemount. He has lived in Apple Valley for 53 years, since before it was an official municipality.

"Nobody on our squad likes to miss being here," says Lilja. "I just love the people and get a kick out of how they treat each other. Being involved with the rifle squad is something you don't want to give up, and I don't want to leave it until I die. Even then, I will still be out here because my wife and I will be buried out here."

Albert V. Spangenberg is "Big Al," but he's not big. He relishes being tabbed with his nickname and tells me about it on my every visit to the Wednesday crew. Whether he's sitting by himself or with others, Albert has a smile or a smirk plastered on his face. On this morning, he asks me if the Twins beat the Angels last night and I say, "Yes, they did, and Santana got the win." Spangenberg is perusing the daily newspapers with Rich Asbury.

"Big Al" grew up in St. Paul and attended St. Agnes High School and graduated in 1953. Spangenberg joined the U.S. Army in 1954 and served until 1956 as a Private First Class. After being trained at Fort Leonard Wood and Fort Sill, Albert mainly drove truck stateside during his tenure and felt bad about never having the opportunity to serve overseas.

He has lived in nearby Maplewood since 1983 and joined the rifle squad in 2004. Spangenberg was in the trucking business for 27 years, spent 10 years working with the railways, and also sold religious articles during his civilian life. Now 82, Albert belongs to Legion Post 452 in Roseville. He tells me that he spent three years on a rifle squad in Motley, near Fort Ripley, where they conducted services at three cemeteries. So Spangenberg was quite familiar with how an honor guard conducted itself.

"I really like being in on the rifle volleys," said "Big Al." "It's truly our honor to honor the dead here, and it's always a pleasure to volunteer. The reason I came out is because our squad leader, Leo Noe, encouraged me to do it; our kids went to school together."

Kenneth G. Tibesar and I greet each other and I ask him if he is related to Rick Tibesar, the former St. Paul policeman

The color guard and rifle squad at Committal Area 2

and hockey official. Sure enough, he's Ken's cousin. I tell Ken that Rick used to referee my college hockey games, and we joke that we get to see him all the time during Wild hockey games at Xcel whenever somebody gets a penalty, as he is the penalty box attendant.

Ken joined the squad in 2014 and easily fits in to whatever role is needed on a particular day, even though he prefers being a rifleman. Now a resident of Hastings, Tibesar grew up in southeast Minnesota and graduated from Plainview High School in 1966. He is a member of Legion Post 98 in St. Paul Park. Ken joined the U.S. Navy in 1967 and served until 1975 and was aboard a Polaris nuclear submarine stationed in Groton, Connecticut, working in missile control throughout the Atlantic Ocean and the Mediterranean Sea. After active duty, he worked for 3M as a computer programmer for 27 years and retired in 2007.

"My uncle, a Korean War vet, was buried here at Fort Snelling," remarks the self-assured Tibesar. "I was just impressed with the whole thing. So, I contacted Leo to see if there was room for me and it all worked out. I enjoy teasing guys about what branch of the service they were in, and I think it is very healthy and keeps things lighthearted."

"The guys are very dedicated to doing the job, and you really feel like you are respecting the family," adds Tibesar, who handles the website for the rifle squads. "As a Vietnam-era veteran, it was tough to see how we were treated. When the first Iraq War began, it was Vietnam vets who said, 'Support your troops,' and ever since, support for the military has been strong and everybody seems to appreciate their service. At a banquet one time, a Brigadier General spoke and he said that the rifle volley salute is just the military's way of notifying God that there is another guy headed to heaven; I really liked that."

On a splendid spring day, I interview three vets who all happen to have last names that start with the letter "B"—Bernard K. Bondurant, Robert B. Bowen, and Thomas H. Bullinger. Bernie Bondurant is a Chicago native but has lived in Bloomington since 1969. Upon graduation from Wells High School in 1965, Bernie enlisted in the Marine Corps as a 17-year-old with his best friend, James Johnson, under the buddy system program.

An E-5 Sergeant in the infantry, Bondurant was in Vietnam for 14 months and was wounded on three occasions. However, he quickly makes it clear that none of them were life-threatening, though his wounds included his back, shoulder, legs, and hand. In fact, he told his Gunnery Sergeant that they should save the Purple Hearts for soldiers who lose limbs. One of those injuries came when his platoon was involved in a battle of hand grenades.

Bondurant worked for Thermo King for many years, involved with refrigeration units for frozen foods. He worked mostly in the materials department in purchasing and was also in the software IT department. Now 69, Bernie joined the rifle squad in 2009 and is a member of VFW Post 295 in South St. Paul and Military Order of the Purple Heart 268.

Articulate and confident, Bernie fends off barbs about being a Marine while being interviewed. He turns to me, smiles, and says, "There are too many of them for me to fight." Bondurant found out about the rifle squad because he golfed with John Sobaski, also a Wednesday member, and John encouraged him to partake. Then, they both talked Mike Hanzal into joining a few years later. Bernie, who usually volunteers as a rifleman, also is a flag-bearer. The former Marine, who volunteered for the Bloomington Fire Department for eight years, also does volunteering for his church, St. Edward's Catholic Church, in his city.

"Volunteering for the rifle squad is the most important one to me of all the volunteering jobs I have done," states Bondurant. "There is nothing like giving back, especially to those who didn't come back. By doing this job, I am honoring them."

As I saunter toward Bob Bowen, he says, "Wait, let me go get my lawyer before I talk with you." Everybody in the vicinity chortles. Bowen is innocent enough, however, and a real nice guy. He was born in St. Paul but grew up in Stillwater and graduated from high school there in 1955. Enlisting in the U.S. Army, Bowen becomes an E-4 rifleman and cook and spent most of his stint stateside, mostly at Fort Riley, Kansas. He then worked 39 years as a local freight truck driver, retiring in 1999 after spending 25 years with Roadway Express.

Bowen, 79, belongs to the same Legion Post, 542 in Roseville, as does Leo Noe. At a Legion meeting, Noe mentioned that there was room on the Wednesday squad, and Bob joined in 1999. He has served as a rifleman, road guard, and flag presenter. In 18 years, Bowen has witnessed a lot of honor guard ceremonies and has seen a lot of emotional scenes.

One in particular stood out. "There was a little kid, probably about four years old, who was probably a great-grandson of the deceased," says the 79-year-old St. Paul resident. "Reminiscent of John Kennedy, Jr., at his dad's funeral, the kid salutes the casket. It's winter time and everybody gets back on the bus and it's dead silent. We all had our hearts in our throat, and nobody said anything because they were all choked up."

Asked about any other memorable moments, Bowen says, "One time, I was presenting the flag to the wife of the deceased, and she just grabbed my hand and wouldn't let go and she had me by a couple of fingers, at least."

Tom Bullinger sports a nicely cropped white beard and a big smile. Tom grew up in central Minnesota and graduated from Pierz High School in 1968. He spent five years in the U.S. Navy, 1969–74, as an E-5 electronics technician and was a Second Class Petty Officer working as a reactor operator. Bullinger was on the same submarine as fellow Wednesday member Ken Tibesar for two years, and after Tibesar joined the squad, he came to observe in the winter of 2014–15.

Now 67, he joined the rifle squad in the spring of 2015 and currently resides in Maple Grove. Normally a flag-bearer, he also enjoys carrying the ceremonial or chrome rifle. Bullinger worked at the Prairie Island nuclear power plant near Red Wing before going back to work on the family farm for 13 years. Finally, he went to college at St. Cloud State at the age of 37 and got his teaching degree. Tom taught in elementary schools in the Osseo School District, generally in science education. Tom is a member of Legion Post 172 in Osseo-Maple Grove.

The father of three and grandfather of nine, the gentlemanly Bullinger says of the rifle squad, "The most memorable services are the ones for which there are few attendees; it's somebody's last farewell, and you feel bad more people aren't there and you wonder about that. That's why we are here for them."

On a breezy and cloudy spring morn, Gary L. Klein, 73, sits down with me to discuss his story. Gary joined the squad in 2006 and generally fills the role of a rifleman. He belongs

William Morris prepares to fire his 1903 Springfield rifle at a service.

to Legion Post 98 in St. Paul Park, near his residence in Cottage Grove, where he has lived for the past 40 years. Gary was raised in St. Paul and graduated from Washington High School. Klein enlisted in the Air Force in 1962 and did a four-year stint as an Airman Second Class aircraft mechanic. The St. Paulite worked mainly on B-52s and KC-135s while on active duty and was stateside for the duration, almost all of it stationed in Marquette, Michigan.

Klein, a thoughtful and pleasant man, was employed for 34 years as a pressman for West Publishing. Retired in 2001, Klein tells a neat story about how he ended up joining the Wednesday squad in 2006. "My wife and I were having our three-year-old granddaughter, Jenna, on an overnight," says Klein. "It was a Monday night, and the next morning, my wife had Jenna on her lap and told her that grandpa should go get a job. Jenna puts her hands on her hip and says, 'Papa, go get a job.' I had known about the rifle squad for about a year, so the next day was Wednesday and I came out to observe, and I started shortly thereafter."

"Everybody knows we are out here to honor the deceased and their families, that is obvious," continues Klein. "It is also very important for us living veterans to have these kinds of groups for companionship and brotherhood, too." Klein adds that he has several relatives buried at Fort Snelling, including his maternal grandfather.

William L. Morris lives on Bald Eagle Lake in White Bear Lake, a community where he has resided for the past 77 years. In fact, he lives just two miles from his childhood home and was employed by the city of White Bear Lake. He worked with the public works department for 30 years and was the street supervisor for part of that time. For 20 of those years, he was also with the fire and rescue units. Bill is a member of Legion Post 168 in White Bear Lake and has been on the Wednesday squad since 2006.

Easy-going by nature, Morris quit high school and enlisted in the Army in 1953 and was in the 82nd Airborne until 1956. A Specialist Fourth Class, he worked in intelligence and operations and was based at Fort Bragg, North Carolina, and Fort Campbell, Kentucky, after jump school training at Fort Benning, Georgia. His 82nd Airborne outfit was readying to go to

Korea when the armistice was signed in late July of 1953, so he remained stateside for the next three years.

Morris, like almost all members of any day's service, is versatile enough to do most roles but generally is a rifleman, presenter, and flag-bearer. The easy-going 81-year-old is glad to venture out to Fort Snelling every week. "My brother John was killed in Korea and he is buried here, so this is a special place for our family and one of the main reasons I am out here. I heard they were looking for guys, and I was able to join up. I used to drive out with Bob Anderson, who was a St. Paul police lieutenant; it has been great, with a lot of dedicated guys."

Robert P. Roth has an impressive silver moustache and a calm demeanor. Bob graduated from Harding High School in St. Paul in 1971, yet another East-Sider on the rifle squad. He has lived in St. Paul his entire life, save for the time he spent in the U.S. Army 1973–76. In fact, he lives on the same street, McLean Avenue, where he grew up. Bob was an E-4 traffic analyst and was stationed in South Korea for much of his tenure. Technically, Roth was in the Army Security Agency, which ceased to exist as of 1976.

A flag-bearer on duty with the Wednesday honor guard, the 64-year-old Roth remains one of the younger members of the overall group. He joined in 2009, just three weeks after he retired from his job with Sara Lee in Roseville, where he worked for 35 years as a maintenance engineer. Bob belongs to Legion Post 577 (Arcade-Phalen) in St. Paul and to at-large VFW Post 15024. Roth's father was buried at Fort Snelling in 1997.

"It's nice to show recognition for those that have served," states Roth, who has a horde of photos of the Fort Snelling cemetery. "It feels good at the end of the day to feel like you accomplished something, that you may have eased the families' sadness. I believe that our honoring them is a blessing, really, to know that the deceased is remembered and appreciated."

Odell R. Zurn is a mellow fellow with a long military resume. He was raised on a farm near Maynard, Minnesota, and after high school, he enlisted in the Army National Guard in 1956 for two years. Next, he joined the Air Force and was on active duty for five years (1958–63). Zurn was a flight engineer on C-130s and as an E-7, he reached the rank of Master Sergeant. Odell was part of the Strategic Air Command, and his main posts were at Bangor, Maine, and Clark Air Force Base in the Philippines.

He then became a part of the Oklahoma Air Guard, then the Minnesota Air Guard, and finally the Air Force Reserve near the airport. His final year of service came in 1982, wrapping up a 23-year career in the branches of military service. He is a member of VFW Post 5555 in Richfield and Legion Post 580 in Chanhassen.

Odell, now 77, joined the squad in 2005, the same year he retired from his job with Northwest Airlines. Zurn worked in aircraft maintenance for 39 years for the local carrier. He has lived in Chanhassen since 2000 after earlier living in Edina for a decade. Normally, the mild-mannered Odell either is a rifleman or a flag-bearer.

"I've had a good life, and I'd been out to funerals at Fort Snelling and witnessed the honor guard," says Zurn. "As soon as I retired, I knew I would be coming out to volunteer, and it's all been worthwhile."

It's a picture-perfect early summer day and Fort Snelling National Cemetery is serene and pristine. Entering the bustling squad room, I learn that there will be 13 funerals this day. Assistant squad leader Mike Hanzal is his usual buoyant self as he helps squad leader Leo Noe into the room. Leo has injured his foot and is using a cane to get around. The other guys gaze out at the window, taking bets on whether another fellow member will be able to park his truck without damaging others.

Theresa A. Winter arrived early on this day because she knew our interview might take a little longer than the average one. Terri is the only woman who currently is a member of the Memorial Rifle Squad at Fort Snelling. She just happened to be the first person I contacted from the squad, requesting information, as she was the overall Commander in 2014. Throughout the process, she has been nothing but professional, courteous, and helpful.

Her road with the squad has not been easy, but she is resolute in her quest to serve. She is the fourth female to join the male-dominated organization. Two of the other women to serve both volunteered for the Thursday squad. Dianne R. Ouradnik served 2005–08 as a bugler, and Tracy Crist also served from 2004–08, so they served for four years together. The other woman, Tracey Digatono, served in 1998 with the Tuesday squad. Winter joined the Monday squad in 2011 and switched to Wednesdays in 2014.

It's not about trying to forge into a guy's world, according to Winter. She became the overall Commander in just three years, and that role is voted upon by fellow squad members, so she earned it. "Let's be truthful, a lot of the guys from the WWII era and Korea grew up in a different time, and there was some pushback because I was a woman," says Winter, within earshot of her fellow Wednesday volunteers. "It was hard to break through the brotherhood, no doubt. Despite the struggles for being accepted, it's become a home for me. I try to keep focused on why I am here—to give back and to help make one of the worst days a family can endure a little better. You can't put a price on what that does for them and how it makes us feel."

Teresa (Wagner-Nytes is her maiden name) grew up in Sheboygan, Wisconsin, and after high school she enlisted in the U.S. Army Reserve at age 17 in 1980. She graduated from basic training at Fort Dix, New Jersey, in a class that was 25%

female, one of the first co-ed classes in the branch's history. Her father, who was in the Army Air Corps in WWII, was a big influence on Terri's desire to go into the military, and his service left a lasting impression on his daughter.

On active duty for nearly six years, Terri was an E-5 cook and then a dental assistant while in the Army. She spent time in her hometown of Sheboygan for a few years before moving on to Fort Ripley and then to the Twin Cities to work for the 5501 Medical Hospital in Minneapolis.

Terri Winter is photographed with her customary chrome rifle. Winter became the first woman to become overall Commander in 2014 and is currently the only woman on the squad.

Following her service, Winter married, had a son (who now lives in Duluth), and had various jobs. Terri worked as a bartender for six years. She has managed dental offices and held other administrative positions, including working with employee benefits. Terri is a fighter and she is tenacious. She went back to college at age 45 at Metro State in St. Paul to pursue a degree in computer forensics science and earned her bachelor's in applied science in 2012.

In 2014, she secured a job at Fort Snelling Cemetery, in part because of her success on the rifle squad. She is a cemetery representative, a liaison between the rifle squad and the family. She represents the staff of the cemetery by preparing all of the documentation for the service, then meeting the family and supporters, and leading the procession to the committal area. Terri works four days a week, at least five hours per day, with a maximum of eight. It's the perfect job, according to her. She says, "It's just an extension of what I do with the rifle squad; you can't teach compassion, it just has to be there."

Winter, who lives in Cottage Grove, belongs to Legion Post 98 in nearby St. Paul Park and to Rosetown Legion Post 542. When on the Monday squad, she was a flag-bearer. With the Wednesday team, she rotates roles but relishes carrying the chrome rifle. Her first foray out to the cemetery came when her brother-in-law, a Marine, passed away at age 40. "It was my birthday, too, and that service had a big effect on me," says Terri. "Bruce Legan, who was on the Monday squad that did the service, was a tutor at the learning center I was attending at the time, and he encouraged me to come out and I ended up starting with them."

Queried about whether or not her demeanor has changed since her arrival, Winter says, "It's a man's world here, so I have to work twice as hard so I don't ruffle any feathers. You have to let some of the stuff slide that I hear; but sometimes, you have to dish it right back so they respect you and know that you will stand up for yourself."

Finally, Winter closes our talk with a story about the first day she was the overall Commander in January of 2014. She was on the Monday squad at the time and WCCO and KARE-11 TV were out to do a segment on that occasion, a day of bitter cold with a wicked wind. A few days later, Winter received a card. The writer explained that she was a 12-year-old girl and was there that day when her grandpa was buried.

"She thanked the entire squad for standing out in the cold and honoring her grandfather," said an appreciative Winter. "It choked me up then and even now, just talking about it. I have a wall of inspiration at home from my time out here, from tributes I have received, and it means a lot."

Eugene E. Wenthold is introduced to me by Terri. He seems at first to be an understated person, and that assessment proves true. Gene is very informative and is an easy interview. Wenthold appreciates the leadership's leeway in allowing him to participate from May until November on the Wednesday squad, as he and his wife sojourn to Mesa, Arizona, as snowbirds each winter. Gene joined the rifle squad in 2006, a year after retiring from a 34-year run as a middle-school art teacher, including 25 years at Scott Highlands and seven at Valley Middle School. He has been an active member of Legion Post 1776 in Apple Valley, where he has resided for the past 45 years, and has been the commander there on five separate occasions.

A native of Decorah, Iowa, Gene graduated from Ossian Central Catholic High School nearby before serving in the U.S. Navy 1963–67. He trained at the Great Lakes Naval Station in Illinois and then attended submarine school in New London, Connecticut. Next, he was on to nuclear power school in California. He was a machinist's mate Third Class and was aboard the USS *DeHaven* 727, a WWII–era destroyer. After two tours in Vietnam, Wenthold matriculated to Mankato State University, where he received his degree in art education in 1972.

"My wife and I will both be buried out here," the 73-year-old Wenthold says. "It is such an honor for all of us to do this service for our fellow service members, from all branches of the service. There are several guys from our Legion who are on the squads, and so we all know about the rifle squads. I found out there was room on Wednesday, and they seemed like a good bunch when I observed, and they took me right away. We provide the same service and thank you from our government; whether or not you were a Private or a General, it doesn't matter. I also appreciate that the cemetery always looks great in tribute to the deceased."

John W. Sobaski has just finished playing cribbage with three other squad members and he saunters over for questioning. When he offers that he will be buried out here in an "ammo can," I'm not sure if he is joking or not. John has been on the Wednesday squad since 2006, the same year that he retired from Marathon Oil Company, where he worked for 33 years as a steam fitter.

Born just a few weeks after WWII ended in September of 1945, John played football, hockey, and track for St. Paul Park High School, graduating in 1964. Drafted in 1965, Sobaski was in the U.S. Army 1965–67 and was an E-5 Sergeant in the infantry.

After training at Fort Lewis in Washington State, Sobaski landed in Vietnam on his 21st birthday with the 4th Infantry Division. Just four hours later, John was standing on a hill and ready for combat, as he was for the next 12 months in the Central Highlands region. Despite heavy action, he was never wounded and developed a strong bond with his platoon, which was made up of guys from Minnesota, Wisconsin, and Missouri. His company has a reunion every three years. Our conversation about Vietnam was intense but very revealing, including comments that you were always on edge and your instincts had to be like an animal's.

"Within a year of my retirement, I knew joining the rifle squad would be the honorable thing to do," says a reflective Sobaski. "I had seen a documentary on the rifle squad and just walked out here on a Wednesday. Being out here has helped me bring closure to my own experiences in Vietnam, especially in regard to buddies who didn't come back. It's my way of saying goodbye to them and honoring them. It's not always easy to share war experiences, except with guys who were there, and I can do that here."

Now 71, Sobaski lives in Hastings after residing in Inver Grove Heights for 24 years. He is a member of VFW Post 295 in South St. Paul and Legion Post 95 in St. Paul Park and normally is a rifleman when on duty. A tough but thoughtful person, Sobaski adds, "These are the nicest guys you could ever meet, and they are committed. There is a lot of teasing, of course, but they are kind and friendly, and we have strong relationships."

In the midst of a cribbage game later, Sobaski tells me a story about a legendary funeral service that has been retold among rifle squad members for years. It appears that a presenter was warning the family and assembled mourners about the impending rifle volleys. An elderly woman, apparently the wife of the deceased, was seated at the end of the bench in the committal area. When the first volley rang out, the woman was startled and pulled back with alarm, holding her chest. A boy about five years old, likely the grandson or great-grandson, shouted out, "They just shot grandma." The guys surrounding Sobaski howled, as did I.

James H. Thompson is a Toledo, Ohio, native who has been a squad member since 2012. Jim's father was a Marine in WWII who fought in the Pacific Theater in such places as Tarawa, Guadalcanal, and Iwo Jima. One brother was in the Army and another in the Air Force. Jim entered the Marine Corps in 1964 and was a corporal in the infantry. While in Quantico, Virginia, for schooling, he met his future wife, Janet, on leave in Washington, D.C., as she was working for the National Security Agency.

Sent to Vietnam, the witty and talkative Thompson says he was there exactly two years, three months, and 10 days. Of his overseas tour, he simply says that he was in heavy combat. His recollection of his time "in country" is not unusual for Vietnam-era veterans. After his four years of active duty ended in 1968, Jim later became a member of the Army Reserve (1970–71). In civilian life, Thompson was employed by the Minneapolis Fire Department. Not surprisingly, Jim says he worked as a firefighter exactly 25 years, three months, and seven days and retired in 2000. The 20-year Lakeville resident belongs to Legion Post 1776 in Apple Valley and VFW Post 5555 in Richfield. He and his wife travel extensively and have been to all 50 states.

"I have a connection to Bob Nelson out at Apple Valley and came out on Wednesday," states Thompson, who usually volunteers as a flag-bearer. "I was on a waiting list for two years but finally caught on. This squad is a lot of fun and is so enjoyable; the camaraderie can't be matched, and we have a lot in common. Being on the rifle squad is the best volunteer thing you can do; we have a good time, but it's also a healing process for the combat veterans."

Michael T. Theisen arrives wearing shorts, but he doesn't receive any guff from his compatriots because they realize he has been dealing with some serious medical issues. He won't be going out with the squad this day but just wanted to let the group know about his status and to be a part of the camaraderie. Still in pain from his most recent surgery, the fast-talking Theisen is definitely an exciting personality.

After exchanging pleasantries with everyone, Mike sits down with me and we find out we were both from large Catholic families and share four brothers who have the same first names. Mike, who grew up in Minneapolis and graduated from Robbinsdale High in 1972, does one-up me because he's from a family of 13 with nine boys while the Hoey's from Taconite, Minnesota, had only 11 children with eight boys. We talk at length about the benefits of being from a big brood before venturing on to the matters at hand.

It becomes clear that Mike is very dedicated to military causes. After high school, Theisen was in the U.S. Army 1972–76 and became a Ranger and a team leader. A Sergeant E-5, Mike had been in Vietnam for a little more than seven months when he was hit by shrapnel. That was the extent of our conversation about his active service. Following his active duty, Theisen was employed by the U.S. Postal Service for 26 years before he retired in 2006 because of pain from his disability.

Theisen, a great storyteller, is a member of Legion Post 361 (Hanson-Anderson) in Denham, Minnesota, and has lived in Brooklyn Park for over 20 years. He joined the Wednesday group in 2008. "I knew that when I left the service, I would have to do something to pay back for those who didn't come back and for my own healing," says Theisen. "Every guy here might have a little different reason for why they do this, but everybody here is a cut above so that families will have a great memory of a great funeral before they have to deal with the grief. These people who volunteer here are among the best guys in the world."

Now 62, Theisen is giving back. For the past 37 years, he has volunteered, in private, to take vets to help them get benefits at the Anoka County Veterans Service Office.

Chapter 10

Monday Squad

My first visit to Monday's squad comes on a cold and windy morning in early February, the day after Super Bowl XLIX. As my blue 1994 Chevy S-10 pulls into the parking lot at the rifle squad's cramped quarters at the Fort Snelling maintenance facility, crews are already busy trimming the hardwood trees and pruning, the optimum time of year for such an endeavor.

I introduce myself to Michael L. Rose, the squad leader since 2014, who is busy organizing for the day's funerals. He is quick to reflect any recognition for himself and is focused on his men, a true leader. It didn't take long for me to figure out that this guy would be someone to be trusted in a tight spot or in a foxhole, to be sure. Rose is an Ohio native and graduated from Hamilton Catholic in 1964.

After high school, Rose enlisted in the Marine Corps, and after training in San Diego and at Camp Pendleton he went for more training in Okinawa. A Sargent E-5, Mike was in the 3rd Marine Division and was sent to Vietnam and was "in country" for 10 months. He knew how to type and was placed in the "combat casualty reporting" unit. Thus, he wrote letters to families of soldiers who were killed, wounded, or missing in action. "It was my main duty over there," said Rose. "Most of the time I did it in a tent."

Following discharge from active duty in 1967, Rose went to Miami of Ohio in Oxford and received a degree in political science in 1971. He worked in state government in Columbus for several years and proceeded to get his PhD in labor relations at the Ohio State University. He then got a job teaching at Drake University (1980–87) in Des Moines, Iowa. When his wife got a job at St. Paul Companies in 1987, they moved to the Twin Cities. Mike then got an associate's degree in computer programming and worked as a consultant for a few years before finishing his civilian career with American Express.

Now 71, Rose belongs to VFW Post 7555 in Roseville, where he has lived for the past 30 years. In 2003, Mike decided to join the rifle squad. "I had seen a story on TV about the rifle squad, and my wife mentioned that I should do it," says Rose. "I called John O'Neill who was on the Monday squad, and he told me to come on out and check us out. I did and got on right away, as they were short some guys at the time."

"Our Monday guys certainly have a good sense of humor, and they are very sociable," remarks Rose on his squad. "They respect each other and don't really complain. They see their volunteering here as a sense of duty; however, I think there is a lot of fulfillment. They get way more out of it than they give."

Between services, Rose gets everybody's attention for a few instructions, but mostly to tell some jokes, and there is always one about the Irish from this Irishman. I conduct interviews in the van as we await the next service, and Mike reads a nice obituary from the *Star Tribune* about a Marine to be buried this day.

Gordon H. Bauer is obviously a revered member of the squad. Even at the age of 92, this easy-going chap is very sharp and quick with a retort to any query. Bauer joined the squad in 2002, 18 years after he retired from a 34-year career working the switchboard with American Telephone and Telegraph. He lives in the Highland Park area of St. Paul. Gordy grew up in the Frogtown area of the city and graduated from Mechanic

The Monday squad is shown before loading the van for another round of funerals in early August of 2017.

Arts High School in 1943.

Enlisting in the Navy right away, Bauer did two stints of active duty, 1943–46 and 1950–52, as he served in both WWII and the Korean War. Gordy was a diesel engineer and was on the USS *West Point*, which carried 8,000 troops and numerous LCMs (Landing Craft, Mechanized) and LSTs (Landing Ship, Tank). After active duty, he joined VFW Post 6690 in Mendota and American Legion Post 98 in St. Paul Park.

A sincerely nice man, Bauer is one of those guys with a perpetual smile and a pleasant demeanor. He is no stranger to volunteering; he also works at the Armed Services Center at the Lindbergh terminal (midnight to 4:00 a.m.) taking care of active duty personnel and has done so since 2002, the same year he joined the rifle squad.

"It's an honor to be here at Fort Snelling," says Bauer. "We enjoy visiting with each other from a social standpoint and have a good time, but we know how to be professional when we are out for the funerals."

Bauer has mainly served as a flag-carrier in his 15-year tenure with the Monday group. He was a Commander at his local VFW. Monday squad leader Paul Longen said they needed help on Monday, so I came out and started right away. I've known Mike Rose for a long time and we're very satisfied with the job he has done."

Thomas C. Goodwin has that look of mischief in his eye. He is quick with a retort and a feigned insult to those military men who never had the good fortune of being in the U.S. Marine Corps like himself. Tom was born in Beloit, Wisconsin, and now lives in Apple Valley, where he has been on the city council for the past 33 years. Now 72, Goodwin joined the Marines in 1965 with six other buddies and was a radio operator at a communications base and spent one year in Vietnam and ended up as a corporal. He wasn't involved in heavy fighting but was shot at a few times. Two of his buddies were wounded, and one ended up being one of the 58,200 Americans killed in Southeast Asia.

Tom became a Monday squad member in 2008. As I interview him, he is vilified for being a Marine by a Navy vet. He turned to me and says with a straight face, "Did you know that the Marines are really the Men's Department of the Navy?"

"I joined the rifle squad to honor the people we're burying, of course," says Goodwin. "It's not about the military, per se, it's about honoring people for simply doing a service for the country. We need to honor all of those soldiers, sailors, and airmen who were on guard for us and who didn't know if anyone cared about them, especially from the Vietnam era." The clever and lean Goodwin, a member of Legion Post 1776 in Apple Valley, continues, "Our commander down there, Eugene Wenthold, was on the Wednesday squad, and he mentioned there was an opening on Mondays. I rode around with them for a while, and they invited me on."

Allan J. Johnson joined both the Monday and Thursday

squads in August of 2006 and is currently the overall Commander of the Memorial Rifle Squad. He is a resident of Hopkins and belongs to VFW Post 425 and Legion Post 320 in that suburb. Al was in the U.S. Navy 1963–67 as a Petty Officer Third Class and is a Vietnam veteran, having served on a ship off the South China Sea. He worked for 21 years for Nordic Ware doing warehouse work, mainly assembly and shipping.

A gregarious man, the 73-year-old Johnson also serves as an assistant squad leader under Mike Rose and otherwise rotates in different roles on the squad. He says, "In 2000, my brother was buried out here, and I was so impressed with what I witnessed, so I knew that I needed to join the group. Everybody comes from different branches of the service, and we give each other a hard time but we respect each other and people are there to help each other in their personal lives, too."

Queried about the dedication of the group, Al remarks, "In the winter of 2013, we had a lot of snow one day and just one burial, but all 24 members were here for that person. That tells you how people feel about their responsibility here. I do two days a week and still have time to play softball two days a week and pickle ball two days a week when softball isn't played. I am the overall Commander of all the squads and do whatever needs to be done to help on the two days I serve. Mike Rose gives very clear instructions about our duties, and everybody is trained in most positions so we are very versatile. Though each day's squad has its own make-up, we want to have as much uniformity as we can in how we conduct the funerals."

When introduced to bugler Robert H. Pellow, I recognize him from his performances at the annual Memorial Day services. An unassuming and classy fellow, Bob is appreciative of my recognition of him but is very modest. In great shape for a gentleman aged 88, Pellow has been on the team for 27 years. On this frigid day, Bob plays "Echo Taps" with fellow bugler Roger Otte after playing a version of *Ave Maria.*

Pellow grew up in northeast Minneapolis and graduated from Edison High in 1947, where he played trumpet in the band. Bob quickly joined the Marine Corps and served for five years. A Corporal in heavy weapons, Pellow fought in combat in the Korean War and earned a Purple Heart at the infamous battle at the Chosin Reservoir. While Bob lived much of his adult life in Brooklyn Park, he now resides in New Brighton and belongs to VFW Post 6587 in Spring Lake Park. He was self-employed after active duty, with most of his years spent in the gasoline and vending businesses.

"I was already on the Monday squad, but our bugler was unable to continue so they needed someone to replace him, and I have been doing it for the past 24 years," says the soft-spoken Marine. "I hadn't played the trumpet or bugle for 40 years until being pressed into service, so to speak. It only took a few weeks to get up to speed and feel comfortable."

Pellow is involved with the Metro Marines and serves as their treasurer and marches in numerous parades, while also serving as a bugler. In summation, Pellow says, "I really enjoy being on the squad. We have a long list of guys who served with us who are now gone, and that is tough."

Marshall D. Peterson is a big man with a big heart. With a cool moustache and a helping demeanor, Marshall is a font of information and an easy interview. He joined the squad in 2012 and mainly serves as a flag presenter. Originally from St. Peter, Minnesota, Peterson worked for the U.S. Postal Service as a mail-carrier for 26 years in Eden Prairie.

Now residing in Maple Grove, the 67-year-old belongs to Legion Post 1982 in St. Paul after a long career in the military. On active duty 1972–75, Peterson was a Lieutenant Commander in the U.S. Navy and then was in the Navy Reserve 1981–94. He served for three years in the Hawaiian Islands and around Midway Island while performing shore duty. He jokes, "Can you believe I was in the Navy in those two spots and did a total of two days at sea on all-day long training cruises? No kidding. It wasn't my choice."

Peterson found out about the rifle squad years before his retirement and wanted to join as soon as he was able. He knows well the importance of conducting the funerals. "There is one funeral that really stands out in regard to how powerful it was," says Marshall. "The gentleman who died was from Pequot Lakes and there was no presence at the funeral by anyone for him. He apparently had no relationships with people, and nobody in the world cared for him, and he had lived in a nursing home the last eight years of his life. The only person at the funeral besides us was the funeral director, and this guy was buried in an unpainted wooden box made out of 5/8" plywood."

"This guy had appeared to have had absolutely nothing," adds a somber Peterson. "However, he left directions on what to do upon his death. He wanted to be buried at Fort Snelling. His flag was then going to be brought back to the nursing home to be flown there. That sums up why we are here; we were here for him." Marshall gulped as he spoke the final words.

Roger L. Otte grew up on a farm near Randolph, Minnesota, and now drives 37 miles from his home in Cannon Falls to serve at Fort Snelling. A self-assured 74-year-old, he has served with fellow bugler Bob Pellow doing their version of "Echo Taps" since 2009. Otte was in the Navy 1964–70 and served stateside as an A-5. He belongs to American Legion Post 142 in Cannon Falls.

The Monday squad is the only one that does extra instrumentals besides "Taps." Standing on the crusty snow and ice a distance from the funeral gathering, Otte played "America the Beautiful" after the U.S. flag was folded and presented to the family. Sometimes they play the anthem of the particular branch the deceased was active in as a serviceman. In fact, they have 30 laminated music cards with notes on a music holder that they use to do different ditties. On this day, it is obvious that the family appreciates their efforts as they nod in their direction.

"I was a pallbearer for a friend who was buried at Fort Snelling," remarks the calm Otte. "I was very impressed with how the honor guard operates and I had also been on a rifle squad in Cannon Falls where we do a few funerals a month. Of course, our group enjoys being together as a social gathering, as we have some very deep and binding relationships. Playing "Taps" is always emotional for people and it stays with you. On many occasions, the last guys walking to get back on the van tell us that we've done it again; that we made the family cry when we played those simple 24 notes of 'Taps.'"

Gary R. Riesenberg joined the rifle squad in 2006 and is rightly proud of his 11 years of service. Appearing much younger than his 69 years, Riesenberg grew up on a farm in St. James, Minnesota, and has lived in south Minneapolis since 1972. Still small in size, Gary was just 5'5" and only 92 pounds when he was drafted and joined the Marine Corps in 1968. It's evident that he relishes being on the squad and loves to be among the guys, even if he is the butt of jokes more than the others.

"The best thing about being out here with these guys is that they understand what it is like to be in the service or to be involved in war and combat," states Riesenberg. "Most of us are out here for a very simple reason—we want to give back to the veterans who served and this is the final thing we can do for them. We also get to do a lot of funerals because we are on Monday and we average 13–15 funerals most days."

Riesenberg was an E-5 Sergeant during his stint in the Marines and served in the infantry. He was one of the famous "tunnel rats," soldiers who had to burrow into claustrophobic spaces in search of the enemy. Gary was fortunate that his 21" waist allowed him to function in those incredibly tight areas; he estimates that he did the extra duty 20–25 times. Riesenberg carried only a pistol, a flashlight, and concussion grenades with him as he traversed the snake-ridden, booby-trapped spaces. He was one of four brothers to serve in Vietnam; all survived their time "in country." Gary was in Vietnam for nearly a year.

His brother Bill was buried at Fort Snelling in 1983. Riesenberg finished active duty in 1970 and spent most of his civilian career supervising carriers for the Minneapolis *Star Tribune.* He has also been an auctioneer for the past 26 years and has served as a volunteer at the Veterans Affairs Medical Center.

James F. Smith joined the Monday squad in 2009. He saw a man at a store with the Memorial Rifle Squad jacket on, and he inquired about the organization and decided it was a worthy endeavor. "It was that simple," says Jim. "He was on the Wednesday squad and told me everything I wanted to know. I'm just sorry I didn't hear about it earlier."

Smith lives in northeast Minneapolis. Mainly a flag-carrier, he belongs to VFW Post 7555 in Roseville and Rosetown American Legion Post 452 in the same city. He was drafted into the Army and served 1964–66, doing a stint in Vietnam in 1965–66. Smith was a Private First Class involved in artillery communication. He had several occupations during his career, highlighted by 10 years at Burlington Northern Railroad and 11 years at Napa Auto Parts.

"It has been very rewarding to be on the squad and you couldn't meet a better bunch of guys," says Smith. "I respect all of them so much, for their active duty and for their willingness to do honor for the deceased veterans. It's all about giving something back; that is so important in life. We aren't in it for the glory."

Timothy J. Zwack could be a one-man public relations firm for the Memorial Rifle Squad at Fort Snelling National Cemetery. Articulate and erudite, the 68-year old resident of West St. Paul (45 years) was strong in his praise for the organization and detailed in his observations. Zwack became a Monday member late in 2010. Tim served in the Army Reserve in

Faribault on the weekends and was a radio repairman as a Specialist 6 and now is a member of Legion Post 542 in Roseville.

Zwack grew up in the Lexington-St. Clair area of St. Paul and graduated from St. Thomas Military Academy in 1966, the first year the all-male military high school was based in Mendota Heights. As a 14-year-old freshman, Tim served as part of the school's honor guard at his grandfather's funeral. His grandpa, Joseph Pazderski, had served in WWI and earned a Purple Heart. After graduating from St. Thomas College in 1970 with a degree in secondary education specializing in English, he enlisted in the Army Reserve in 1970 and served for six years. Tim spent 34 years as a purchasing agent for family-owned Gross-Given Manufacturing and retired in 2006.

"Every facet of what we do as an honor guard is important," says Zwack, who folds and presents flags when a traditional casket is present. "But folding and presenting the flag is critical because you are face to face with the family. We have a 'canned' statement that we give them, of course, but sometimes we say the presentation and it is extremely personal. The toughest ones for me are the ones where there is hardly anyone present."

The most memorable funeral he presided at concerned a former St. Thomas Academy English teacher named James Keane in late 2014. Zwack says, "I saw his name on the schedule, and I was fortunate to be the presenter at the burial. I told his widow that he was one of my favorite teachers, and there was an audible gasp that came from the other family members, according to others who were present there. He was an influential teacher in my formative years. In fact, he was the teacher who announced to our English class that President Kennedy has been assassinated, and he was very comforting."

Two other funerals made a big impact on Zwack, too. One involved a different day of the week, where Tim was allowed to be the presenter for his uncle's funeral. Another involved a large gathering. Zwack noticed what appeared to be 8–10 grandchildren of the deceased, who were impeccably dressed and well-mannered. "They were probably all about 12–16 years old, and they were just very attentive and definitely moved by the ceremony for their grandfather. You could just see they were affected by the funeral, and their presence and demeanor were just a real tribute to their grandpa."

It's no secret why Tim Zwack joined the service or joined the Memorial Rifle Squad. He quickly gives me a rundown of his family's military service without missing a beat. It was his duty to honor their service. He lists the names of 13 uncles who had served in WWII and where they served, mostly in the Army and Navy. He mentions his grandpa Joe, who earned a Purple Heart in France during WWI; his father-in-law, who was in the Battle of Midway in 1942; and his brother-in-law and his son-in law.

On my next sojourn to confer with the Monday squad as winter begins to wane, I visit with six or seven others. Once again, this group proves to be efficient and professional in manner as they conduct 11 funerals. Several members are still off as snow-birds, strewn between Arizona, Texas, and Florida. The banter is mostly about the Minnesota Wild's struggles on the ice and the upcoming NCAA basketball tournament before we venture out in the damp air.

Marc E. Anderson is a 71-year-old who lives in Burnsville. Marc joined the squad in 2014 and has primarily served as a flag-carrier and rifleman. He was raised in Rosemount and graduated from that southern suburb in 1964 before spending three years at North Dakota State University. Drafted into the Army after quitting school, Anderson served 1968–71 as a First Lieutenant. He spent a year in Vietnam and saw heavy combat, earning a Bronze Star for his heroics.

Following active duty, after earning degrees in both biology and chemistry from Mankato State University, he spent 40

Marc Anderson (left) and Bob Peterson (right) at attention.

years in business management, including 10 for the Minnesota Vikings and 10 for Ecolab. Anderson belongs to VFW Post 210 in Lakeville, where he is the service officer and the poppy chairman. Since his retirement from the business world, Marc has also volunteered for the DAV and the homeless.

He adds, "I joined the squad because I wanted to give back, like all the other guys. I am proud to be a Vietnam veteran, but for many years I kept it under the vest. It was tough to see us get the treatment we did in the 1970s and 1980s. That has all changed now, and I think the Vietnam vets are really feeling respected. It is nice to work through the emotional challenges by sharing experiences with other guys who were there. I just love coming here every week to be with our group to honor the fallen."

George J. Gonzalez of Maplewood (23 years) grew up in Pennsylvania and served in the U.S. Army 1965–67. A Specialist Fourth Class, Gonzalez did duty with the Old Guard at

Arlington National Cemetery so serving with the Memorial Rifle Squad seems an appropriate volunteer activity for him. He says, "It was sad duty because I was a driver for the families who were burying their loved ones and it was starting to get real busy when I was there as the casualties were really mounting."

"It's very gratifying to hear some of the guys on the squad share some of their experiences from their service," says the engaging 72-year-old, who retired from his civilian job in 2013 in customer management with 3M for a whopping 45 years. "No one else really knows what they go through, especially those who were involved in the heavy fighting. I had seen a TV story on the squad it showed them on a day when it was bitterly cold and I thought that was true service. I went on the Internet and researched them and got on a waiting list for seven months and eventually got on in August of 2014. It's a real honor for me to do this job, and I feel better than when I was doing this during my active duty. This time, I know that the people who died lived a lot longer life."

Robert E. Peterson, an enthusiastic and upbeat resident of Maple Grove, is a 67-year-old former Army veteran. He grew up in south Minneapolis and graduated from Roosevelt in 1967. Serving as a Specialist Fourth Class, Peterson enlisted and served 1968–71 and was trained as an air traffic controller. A quipster, he says, "After training at Fort Rucker in Alabama, they sent me to Germany to spy on the Russians."

A member of Legion Post 435 in Richfield, Bob got an education degree from the University of Minnesota and spent 25 years as a deputy with the Hennepin County Sheriff's Department. Since joining the squad in 2007, Peterson has served mainly as a rifleman, and he makes it clear that there is great misinformation regarding the so-called 21-gun salutes.

"There is no such thing as a 21-gun salute," says Peterson. "There are three rifle volleys no matter how many men are firing rifles. We must have a minimum of five and a maximum of eight, so we could have 15 or we could have 24."

"I've wanted to volunteer with the rifle squad for a long time," adds Bob. "My dad was a Navy vet who was in the Philippines, but he never talked about his time in the military. I was inspired by the book *Band of Brothers* and what they did, and I wanted to pay my respects by doing this. I remember a different time during the Vietnam era when some of our officials told us not to wear our military uniforms when we flew home for fear of being identified as a serviceman. I am glad that attitude has changed."

"There is a necessity for all of our squads to act uniformly in how we conduct our honor guards," says Peterson. "We have and will continue to be a model for developing other rifle squads. I know that our Monday group does things the right way. Wayne Pickett, a Marine, set the tone for our group as our squad leader; he was the nicest guy and has passed away. He had been captured by the Chinese in the Korean War and was a prisoner-of-war for 999 days."

Michael P. Zerr was drafted but enlisted in the U.S. Army in 1968, at the height of the Vietnam War. He was raised in Harvey, North Dakota. Mike was a helicopter mechanic and was in country in Vietnam for 15 months, just seven miles from the Cambodian border. Following active duty, Zerr repaired cars and locomotives for the Soo and Canadian Railroad for 33 years. He has lived in Cottage Grove since 1987 and has been the Commander at VFW Post 8752 there for six years.

"Being on the rifle squad is not work, whatsoever," states Zerr. "It's an honor to be doing this and a privilege. Like most people, I rotate doing different jobs on the squad but I really like being a flag-carrier. I was well aware of the squad when I was working and was intent on joining them after I retired. I am just hopeful that there will be someone here for me when it is my turn to be buried here."

Donald D. Menier, one of many rifle squad members who grew up on the St. Paul's East Side, has been on the Monday squad since 2013 and is a member of American Legion Post 542 based in Roseville, where he is a resident. Now 74, the kind Menier was in the Army Air Corps 1961–64 after graduating from Harding High School. Don was a Specialist 5 and a helicopter mechanic, serving stateside at five posts during his three-year stint. After active duty, he was involved in property management and spent many years with Wellington Management.

"I can't think of another thing I would do on a Monday morning than be here to serve at these funerals," says the reserved Menier.

Don Menier, a rifleman on Mondays, smiles amid the banter on the van.

"I came out here and put my name in to serve on one of the squads, and the only opening was on Monday. It more than met my expectations and it has been unbelievably wonderful. I am saddened that I didn't do it 10 years earlier. We are brothers in arms, and I love this squad and what we do. They'll have to carry me out before I'm done here. I also have some really good buddies who serve on Wednesday."

Menier currently serves as a rifleman, and his loyalty to the rifle squad is evidenced by the tattoo on his back, which is the rifle squad's emblem. At least, that is what I have been told!

With the trees in full bloom on a gorgeous spring day, spirits are high as the squad members trickle in for duty on a day with 15 funerals slated. Amidst scintillating banter, I sit down with Francis E. (Fran) Buesgens, a 10-year member of the squad. A thoughtful gent, Fran taught elementary school (grades 4–6) in the Mounds View School District for 29 years and has lived in that suburb for 31 years. After graduating from Belle Plaine High School in 1964, Buesgens was drafted into the Army and did basic training at Fort Campbell, Kentucky, and served for two years as a member of the Military Police. He did physical security for munitions at the Army depot at Seneca, New York.

A member of American Legion Post 513 in New Brighton, Buesgens saw a story on television about the rifle squad during his teaching career and figured he would join when convenient. "My active duty was rather easy and I felt a little guilty that I wasn't in any danger, really," says the 70-year-old St. Cloud State alum. "This is a way I can pay back and give reverence to the guys who were in combat. Eight of my uncles were in the service, and my dad was in the Army in WWII and fought in both North Africa and Italy. Three of my uncles are buried here, and my godfather, too."

Buesgens adds, "I work the flags but have also done some work on the rifles and also with presenting. The toughest part of any funeral for me is to see the kids, especially as a teacher of young children. We learn a lot on the bus and in the squad room about the service of all these guys and about their personal lives, too, and it is amazing."

James F. Kirby has served on the Monday squad since 2003 and primarily serves as a rifleman. Kirby grew up in Bradley, South Dakota, and attended a country school. He smiles broadly and says that he was the salutatorian in his class, which totaled three people. Jim giggles. A smart and gentlemanly type, Jim immediately then served in the Marines 1953–56; most of that time was spent in Korea. Reaching the rank of Sergeant, Kirby was a radar technician.

Following active duty, Jim worked for Univac for 10 years and then 26 years for Rosemount Corporation, where he was the director of research and development. He has lived in Burnsville for over 50 years and belongs to VFW Post 5247 out of Dawson, Minnesota.

"Bob Pellow had told me about the rifle squad, and so I came out with the Monday group and was able to join up right away," says Kirby, now 82. "We have a pretty unique bunch of guys." He looks at the vets surrounding him and says, "There are a few jerks, of course." Everybody bursts out laughing, and the guffaws, catcalls, and jokes emanate from throughout the room.

Kirby is still in touch with his senior drill instructor from basic training, who is now 84 and still living in California. He is also proud that he is one of three brothers to serve in the Marines, along with three nephews. Interestingly enough, Jim was able to present the funeral flag at the funeral of his junior drill instructor in Madison Lake, Minnesota, in 2015.

Queried about an anecdote about any of the funerals he has witnessed, Kirby retorts, "There was one that would be tough to top. Apparently, there was a vet who had been a baker, and believe it or not, his last name was Baker. His wife baked his ashes into a round three-tier cake and I swear to God she put that cake in an urn to be buried. That's a true story."

Paul R. Longen, 81, has been retired for 19 years from Honeywell, where he worked as an electronic technician for 38 years. Longen, who lives in Minneapolis, graduated from South High School in 1953 and is in his 16th year with the Monday contingent. Paul served in the U.S. Navy 1954–58 as an electronics mate. Newport, Rhode Island, served as his home port during his tenure but he spent much of his time patrolling the Mediterranean Sea.

"One of my shipmates, Al Jelinek, worked on the Friday squad and he urged me to come out," says Longen, who served as a squad leader for Monday for three years. "Wayne Pickett was the squad leader before me, and he succeeded Dennis Christy, who started the Monday squad in 1979. Christy was a WWII vet and was in an artillery company and spent the entire time in Europe. He was a great guy. Mike Rose is only the fourth leader for Monday."

A member of VFW Post 7555 in Roseville, Longen has done various duties on the squad but currently is a flag-holder. An interesting chap with a great memory, Longen encourages me to get together with Glenn O'Malley, a charter member of the rifle squad who knows a lot of the history of the rifle squad, when he visits in July.

Kenneth W. Gibson joined the rifle squad in 2015, and he is one of three fellows, along with Allan Johnson and Andrew Urness, who do service two days a week. Ken grew up on St. Paul's East Side and attended Harding High but left as a junior at age 17 during the summer of 1960 to join the Navy. He was a boiler tender aboard the USS *Kearsage*, an aircraft carrier that cruised the Pacific. While serving in Long Beach, California, the *Kearsage* was parked alongside the infamous "Spruce Goose," and Gibson's crew finagled a tour of Howard Hughes's legendary aircraft and found it was actually made out of real spruce wood. Gibson served for four years as a boiler-tender fireman.

Following his exit from the Navy in 1964, Gibson utilized the GI bill to get his engineering degree and obtained additional training at Univac. Ken spent 31 years at 3M and also worked at Control Data and Montgomery Wards. Interviewed a few days after his 74th birthday, the affable Gibson tells me that he is proud to be a self-taught bugler and enjoys serving in that capacity but also serves as the van driver, a rifleman, and a flag-bearer. He had recently passed the test and is now an official member of Bugles Across America, meaning he can play "Taps" for any veteran's service in the Twin Cities area.

The Monday squad gathers in the squad room with squad leader Mike Rose (far right of those standing).

"There is a lot of camaraderie on both squads, but serving on Mondays and Fridays is certainly different," says the friendly and helpful Roseville resident. "I was in the color guard at the Roseville Legion 542 so I was aware of what role we play. I started with the Monday squad and decided I wanted to serve an additional day and joined the Friday group in 2016. I will be buried here and so will my wife. We are definitely a military family, and Fort Snelling is where my mom and dad are buried, along with a brother and brother-in-law, as well as aunts and uncles and grandparents."

Andrew J. (Jerry) James grew up in Prescott, Wisconsin, and is two days from celebrating his 71st birthday. A low-key man characterized by those surrounding him as simply a nice guy, Jerry joined the rifle squad in 2012. He lives in Lake Elmo after living in adjacent Oakdale for 26 years and is a member of VFW Post 1350 in North St. Paul. James retired from Fairview Health Services as a business manager and worked at several different jobs in the finance field.

James enlisted in the Marine Corps in 1967 as a 21-year-old and was trained in aviation ordnance. He spent 12 months in Vietnam in 1968–69 serving on the personal security force for the U.S. Ambassador to South Vietnam in Saigon. Following his tour in Southeast Asia, he worked at the U.S. Embassy in Bogota, Colombia.

"My father, a WWII Marine, was buried here in 1990, and I thought about being on the rifle squad at that time," recalls James, who serves as a rifleman on the Monday squad. "It was always my intention to eventually serve, and I found out there was an opening with the Monday group. There are a lot of guys from the Vietnam era here now, and that makes it nice because we can identify with each other."

"It is a privilege to be out here to serve our former servicemen and their families," states James, who turns to tell Rose that he will be leaving early today so he can bring his 99-year-old mother to a doctor appointment. "Though we tease each other a lot, we have good cohesion in working together." He then winks and tells me that working the Monday squad is great, too, because they get the Monday federal holidays off.

A few days before I met him in person with his sidekick Gary Riesenberg, I called Roger E. Lippold on his cell phone, and an hour later, I had run out of ink and notepads. An incredibly dynamic personality, Lippold proved to be a fascinating interview and an unforgettable character. Roger is a 72-year old former Air Force Sergeant who joined the Monday squad in 2005.

Lippold was born on an Army Air Force base in Avon, Florida, and went to high school in Eau Claire, Wisconsin. His father flew into the midst of the bombing at Pearl Harbor on December 7, 1941, on a B-17 and spent 18 months in the Pacific fighting the Japanese. Roger served in the Air Force 1964–68 and worked on the Minuteman missiles, B-52s, and in the space shuttle system. Each question to this firebrand is met with a whirlwind of information. Lippold was in a 25-man working group (five-man teams) in Minot, North Dakota, as they were at the forefront of the emerging missile systems and taught by the top computer people in the world.

"I joined the Air Force for four reasons," says Lippold. "To see the world, chase girls, drink beer, and not to have to go to school. I guess I accomplished that, as I only had to take five weeks of basic training before they found out I could help them with the missiles. I worked on maintenance, and many of the people who taught me never had a college degree, but they knew how to think. If you had the talent and the smarts, they could use you, and it didn't matter whether or not you went to school or where you went."

Asked about why he joined the rifle squad, Lippold replied, "I had never been to the cemetery before but a member of my church was one of the original guys on the squad, and he told me about it. I came out on a Monday and met Gordy Bauer and Wayne Pickett, and they were real gems. They decided to let me join them."

Upon arriving at the squad room two days later, Lippold sidles up to buddy Gary Riesenberg and the fun begins. Both are small in stature, but both are big eaters of the ever-present doughnuts, about which they get hounded incessantly. Roger usually works parking cars or as a rifleman when he isn't ri-fling one-liners at his compatriots. He admits that "When the guys get to the squad room, it's like we go back 30 or 40 or 50 years as younger guys."

The father of five children, Lippold still rides his motor-cycle (a 2002 Super Glide) cross-country and plays racquet-ball and golf regularly when he isn't pistol-shooting. This is the third time he has lived in Minnesota, and he currently lives in Brooklyn Center, where he has been for the past 39 years. He worked for AT&T for 24 years, where he was in technical support for computer software systems and retired in 2005.

"Once you join the rifle squad, they are a part of your family, and it becomes an obligation to stick with your buddies," says a serious Lippold. "You get really attached to these guys and when they leave because of illness, inactivity, or death, it's tough on all of us."

Andrew Urness, Jr., is one of only three veterans who serve on two days of the week, along with Allan Johnson (Monday and Thursday) and Ken Gibson (Monday and Friday). Urness, who also serves on the Friday squad, started on Mondays in 1991 and added Fridays in 2002. Andy, a likeable sort, relishes the camaraderie of both days and acknowledges each have a different chemistry.

"In the 26 years I have been with the Monday squad, we have had four real good squad leaders—Dennis Christy, Wayne Pickett, Paul Longen, and now Mike Rose," says the understated Urness. "I've been with Bob Pellow all those years; he's a good friend and we have marched in a lot of parades together, too." When the Friday squad was shorthanded, George Weiss asked him if he could help out, and the easy-going Urness gladly obliged. He says, "No doubt, the two days have a different demeanor, but there are good guys on both and it's nice to say that I have good friends on each."

While he grew up in Iowa, Andy has lived in St. Paul since 1956 and worked for 34 years with Univac as a production engineer. Urness joined the Navy in 1949 and was on active duty until 1951 and then joined the Navy Reserve and was called up 1952–54. He was a storekeeper aboard the destroyer USS *Bryce Canyon* off the coast of Japan after a year in Norfolk, Virginia. He went to technical school in Chicago for two years on the GI bill.

A member of VFW Post 1296 in Richfield, Urness has been a rifleman for 24 of his 26 years on the memorial rifle squads. He found about the organization from his wife. She was working in a drugstore in St. Paul, and a fellow who frequented the place started to tell her about it; he had been a prisoner of war in WW II and was a big supporter of the group. This exchange with his wife prompted Andy to investigate and eventually join.

Ronald J. Snyder is back on his third tour of duty with the Monday squad since 2010 after dealing with numerous illnesses and injuries. The 74-year-old is yet another squad member who grew up on the east side of St. Paul and played hockey for Johnson High coaching legend Rube Gustafson. Upon graduation in 1960, Snyder enlisted in the Air Force and spent four years in active duty. An Airman First Class, Snyder was in the U.S. Security Service, an intelligence branch of the service. He was overseas for three years in both Europe and Asia, involved in radio communications and tracking individuals with the top-secret agency.

Snyder, who has lived in Woodbury for 44 years, belongs to Legion Post 98 in nearby St. Paul Park. After earning his business degree from the University of Minnesota, Ron worked as a vice president for TCF Bank and for 15 years as an agent for the Federal Deposit Insurance Corporation, a job he absolutely loved. Since joining the Monday squad, he has most enjoyed carrying the Air Force flag.

"The Marines on the squad tell me that because I'm an Air Force guy I can't shoot, and they're right because I was an incredibly lousy shot in basic training," says a laughing Snyder. "I am so proud of what we do out here and what all these guys did in service of their country while on active duty, too. I mean, some of these older guys from the WWII era can hardly walk and yet they are still out here serving."

"I had a rather interesting way of finding out about the rifle squad," adds Snyder. "I was retired and working part-time for Walser Buick and met a guy named Gerald Smith, who had been wounded in Korea and was on the rifle squad. His health wasn't good and he wanted someone to replace him on Mondays and that's how I ended up here."

On an idyllic summer day, there are to be 16 funerals. With squad leader Mike Rose prepping for the day's activities starting a bit earlier at 9:30 a.m., I'm hoping to interview two fellows who I have missed on several previous visits. Sure enough, they arrive within a few minutes of each other—Tom Osborne and Duane Van Vickle.

Thomas H. Osborne steps out of his vehicle with a noticeable limp, a problematic left knee that he injured while hiking on the famous Appalachian Trail the last few months. Tom is greeted with firm handshakes, smiles, and wise-cracks from his Monday brothers and it's obvious that he is well-liked and respected by his peers. His positive spirit is apparent, and I quickly learn that he is also a former Iron Ranger. His father was from Hibbing and was in both the Merchant Marine and the Army. Tom graduated from Hibbing High in 1968 after spending his early years in Long Beach, California, where his parents lived for 20 years.

Tom matriculated to the University of Minnesota and finished six quarters there before joining the U.S. Army in 1970. After basic training at Fort Bragg, North Carolina, Osborne went to helicopter school at Fort Rucker, Alabama. He was an E-4 and worked in flight operations and as a door gunner on helicopters while in Vietnam. He became 70% combat disabled after his experience there and suffers from post traumatic stress disorder.

Upon his return to civilian life, Osborne returned to the Iron Range and worked for three years for a construction firm in the taconite plants. He moved to the Twin Cities in 1976 and proceeded to spend the next 37 years working in heating, ventilation, and air conditioning for different companies in the metro area.

The color guard and rifle squad march back to the van after a service.

"The reason I joined the rifle squad out here is because I wanted to make sure that nobody would get treated the way the Vietnam vets were treated when they came back," says Osborne, who has lived in Minneapolis for the past 31 years and joined the squad in 2013. "I carry flags, also do presenting, and I enjoy being up close with the family and being strong for them during this difficult time for them."

For the past five years, the affable Osborne has volunteered at the Veterans Affairs Medical Center on Tuesdays 7–11 a.m., mainly working as an escort and providing information to visitors. He also spent three years working for the Armed Services Center at the Lindbergh Terminal at the airport as a volunteer. Tom belongs to Legion Post 526 in Golden Valley and VFW Post 246 in Minneapolis and is a life member of each. Osborne relates that his VFW Post, located at Lyndale Avenue and 29th Street, is the last surviving post in the mill city.

As for his penchant for hiking, Osborne says, "I have been

hiking the Appalachian for the past three years, and there are a lot of military guys walking that trail. It's 2,200 miles long and I have now finished about 1,450 miles of it—from the start in Springer, Georgia, to the New York/Connecticut border. I have run 10 marathons, including two Grandma's and two Twin Cities, but hiking the Appalachian is much harder than running a marathon. First of all, you are carrying a pack weighing 25–30 pounds with all your gear in it, and then you have to deal with rocks and roots and slippery conditions with rain and it can be very dangerous."

Osborne, who says he is on the trail 8–10 hours a day, hikes with a guy from Costa Rica who is a former serviceman. "It is tough doing this day after day, and you need a lot of fortitude. It's all worth it, though, because it's for a cause. I wear a t-shirt with the words 'I RUN FOR DISABLED VETERANS' emblazoned on the front."

Duane D. Van Vickle is a bull of a man, which is a good thing, because he deals with back and leg issues requiring cortisone shots. Duane, suffering from sciatica for months, is back with the Monday squad and is happy to be back despite the pain. Van Vickle was awarded a Purple Heart in Vietnam, where he spent 13 months in the infantry as a radio man in the Marine Corps. He was wounded during the infamous siege of Khe Sahn by a grenade. Duane enlisted two months after graduating from Edison High in Minneapolis in 1967.

Van Vickle visited the Vietnam Memorial in Washington, D.C., in 2000. "When I saw the Memorial, I knew I wanted and needed to do an honor guard or some type of service out at Fort Snelling," says the 68-year-old, who effuses regular-guy status. "Quite a few of my friends and comrades are on that wall." Duane retired in 2013 after spending more than 42 years with Northwestern Bell in Minneapolis, where his career was spent during numerous jobs. He continues to live in northeast Minneapolis and belongs to Legion Post 555 in that community.

Tom Osborne of the Monday squad met him and told him all about the rifle squad. "I had time to give back after retirement, and it is so nice to be able to talk about your military experiences with these guys," Duane says. "They tell the truth and can identify with you. I'm amazed at some of the active duty time put in by some of the older guys from WWII and Korea. As miserable as I was in Vietnam, it doesn't compare to the heat and cold those guys dealt with."

"I like the fact that we are always busy on Mondays with a lot of funerals," says Van Vickle, who joined the Monday squad early in 2016 and usually is a flag-bearer. "That means we are giving honor to more veterans and giving them the respect and honor they deserve. Everybody on the squad is very friendly and guys feel free to open up about their personal lives. We know we can trust each other."

I interviewed Bruce J. Legan on a hot and humid summer morning when the temperature would rise into the 90s with a dew-point of 70 later in the day. As the fellows groan about the plight of the Twins' pitching staff and wonder if the air conditioning will hold up on the bus, a calm and friendly Legan relates his story. Bruce spent eight years (1987–95) in the Army National Guard in both Kansas and Louisiana.

A 1970 graduate of St. Paul Highland Park, where he excelled in academics, Legan still lives in the Highland area. Now 65, Bruce once played semi-pro tennis. This guy is no dummy, as evidenced by his three degrees in math (B.A. from the University of Minnesota, master's from Oklahoma State, and PhD from Kansas State). He parlayed that into a long career in education. Much of it was done as an adjunct professor at the University of Minnesota (2003–10), Metro State (10 years), St. Thomas University, Inver Hills and North Hennepin Community Colleges, and Hennepin Technical School.

Legan joined the Monday squad in 2006 and has served mostly as a flag-bearer, even though he was still teaching night school at the U of M. His father, who was in the Army Air Corps in World War II and the Air Force during the Korean War, was buried at Fort Snelling in January of 2006, and the younger Legan was impressed.

"It was the first time I had witnessed the rifle squad perform," says Legan. "I joined up shortly thereafter. I think their presence really enriched my dad's funeral because everybody was feeling pretty low. We all knew how important the military was in his life, and the rifle squad helped bring relief to the family."

At a table nearby, the subject of leadership comes up, and I ask three members of the squad about their thoughts on their Monday squad leader. Marshall Peterson says, "Mike Rose is a damn good leader and he reads people very well. Jerry James adds, "You always know where you stand with him and we all appreciate that." Gary Riesenberg states, "Mike has been outstanding and very fair."

Chapter 11

Roster and Memoriams

Founder and Co-Founders (June 19, 1979)

George J. Weiss, Jr.,
U.S. Marine Corps, VFW

Frank J. DeMay,
U.S. Air Force, American Legion

Lawrence J. Pluta,
U.S. Navy, Fleet Reserve Association

Robert L. Anderson,
U.S. Army, VFW

James D. Stewart,
U.S. Navy, Fleet Reserve Association

Joseph J. Nicosia,
U.S. Army, Military Order of Purple Heart

Charter Members*

Dennis H. Christy	Joseph N. Jasper
Richard E. Clancy	James F. Lang
Anthony C. Cuff	Glenn E. O'Malley
Carl A. Falkowski, Sr.	Edward E. Rosander
Raymond V. Frisvold	Alfred P. Schaeppi
Russell R. Green	Melvin S. Schofield
Dean S. Hamre	Robert B. Swanson
Wallace J. Herron	Neville E. Wagoner
Lloyd B. Isaacson	Wilfred J. Weber
Lloyd J. Jackson	William H. Wright

* an additional group of veterans who became charter members in accordance with by-laws that were adopted on January 23, 1980

Squad Commanders

Allan J. Johnson – 2017

Michael L. Pluta – 2016

Richard T. Geis – 2015

Theresa A. Winter – 2014

Daniel J. Fisher – 2013

Gregory A. Rollinger – 2012

Robert H. Nelson – 2011

Archie W. Hazzard – 2010

Timothy J. Gabrio – 2009

Gordon L. Carlson – 2008

Clarence L. Dick – 2007

Theodore A. Nemzek – 2006

Bernie R. Melter – 2005

George Weiss, Jr. – 2003–04

Mark H. Jessen – 2003

John L. O'Neill, Jr. – 2002

Daniel O. Winsjansen – 2001

Wallace J. Herron – 2000

Hugh E. Vasatka – 1999

Peter L. Buie – 1998

Glenn E. O'Malley – 1997

Raymond V. Frisvold – 1996

Kevin E. Burns – 1995

Richard E. Clancy – 1994

Lloyd J. Jackson – 1993

Kenneth K. Tjosvold – 1992

Oliver C. Pederson – 1991

Kenneth E. Nelson – 1990

Chester E. Danielson – 1989

Albert C. Grenz – 1988

Charles S. Fouzie – 1987

Charles P. Korlath – 1986

James F. Lang – 1985

Albert P. Schaeppi – 1984

Dennis H. Christy – 1983

Neville N. Wagoner – 1982

George J. Weiss, Jr. – 1980–81

Inactive Members

Monday Squad

Paul R. Anderson (2007-10)

Bruce Bjornstad (1993-98)

Richard Cole (2004-08)

Michael Demann (2002-06)

Ed Fansler (1998-99)

Edwin Forse (1987-96)

David W. Goodell (2007-15)

David J. Lilja (2008-16)

Michael Martin (2005-08)

Edward L. Mays (1998-98)

Glenn O'Malley (1979-2010)

Ronald Pearson (2002-02)

Merlin Schank (2006-10)

Fred Schauer (1984-86)

Lance Twedt (2006-08)

Earl Witcraft (2003-09)

Tuesday Squad

Virgil Achtenberg (2002-02)

Barry S. Berg (2014-16)

John Biedrzycki (2003-06)

Kermit R. Bischoff (1993-2013)

Al Boettscher (1984-86)

Michael J. Brand (2007-08)

Michael Davis (1979-79)

Tracey Dignatono (1998-98)

Jerry Eide (1979-79)

Russell V. Ek (1979-79)

Donald H. Flynn (1992-2003)

Leslie Fursetzer (1988-94)

Kenneth J. Hall (2010-14)

Archie W. Hazzard (2000-15)

Mike Honeycutt (2003-06)

Mark Jessen (2002-03)

Harry J. Kirchberg (2011-14)

Clarence J. Kraemer (1991-2015)

Donald Kritzeck (1979-79)

Larry Miller (2003-06)

George Olbering (1979-79)

Martin G. Pavek (1996-2016)

Francis Scott (1979-79)

Leon E. Simon (1993-2006)

Theodore J. Stamos (2002-14)

Eugene R. Svendsen (1996-96)

Joseph B. Winter (1997-2008)

Joseph W. Zakrzewski (2010-14)

Wednesday Squad

Robert L. Anderson (2003-09)
Todd B. Benson (2003-06)
Raymond Damkaer (2004-05)
Stanley Eayrs (1998-99)
Philip Groebe (1993-2011)
Loren R. Kramer (2006-15)
John G. Leonard (2001-2012)

Arnold Malaske (1994-98)
Raymond J. Menge (2005-09; 2013-15)
Brian Rohr (2002-06)
Ronald D. Root (2008-11)
Richard F. Rufppe (unknown)

Thursday Squad

Jerry Abeln (2004-04)
Harold J. Brick (1991-2011)
Tracy Crist (2004-08)
Gary D. Erickson (2009-12)
Gary J. Erickson (2009-13)
Bruce Halverson (2012-13)
Robert A. Hanson (1994-2013)
Frank A. Humphrey (1991-98)
George D. Hunkins (1996-2013)
Richard M. Jacquemart (2009-09)
Ken Kauffman (2002-08)
Clarence Kraemer (1991-2015)
Timothy I. Mahoney (2008-09)
Gary E. May (2009-09)
Pierre J. Nadeau (2000-13)

George F. Nelson (2007-09)
John Ohotto (2013-16)
Daniel Ojeda (2003-03)
Robert O'Neil (1984-87)
Dianne R. Ouradnik (2005-08)
Thomas Pedersen (2005-16)
Bennie Reich (1998-2006)
Robert Rignell (2001-11)
Patrick Tallarico (2007-08)
Salvatore Tallarico (2008-12)
Ted Thone (1991-2004)
Ivar Tveter (1991-96)
Gordon Young (1988-2002)
Forrest Zemlicka (1998-2002)
Sy Zimmer (1984-90)

Friday Squad

Josh Beatty (2004-04)

Larry L. Buberl (2007-11)

Geoffrey J. Carman (2008-10)

Mike Clark (1998-2003)

Richard F. Cruz (2004-11)

Quentin DeNio (2000-16)

Lester Fournier (1985-87)

Tim Gabrio (2003-16)

Harold A. Goerdt (1998-2016)

Richard S. Gwynn (2014-16)

Brandon (Stu) Kunzer (2004-05)

Allen Moller (2005-16)

Walter J. Muchlegger (1998-2007)

Charlies D. Paige (2011-15)

Daniel S. Petrosky (2009-14)

Paul Rishavy (1993-2012)

Gene L. Schultz (2000-16)

Robert T. Thompson (2003-06)

Deceased Members (In Memoriam)

Name	Date of Death	Organization	Squad	Branch
Michael J. Abrams	Feb. 14, 1999	VFW 6587	Monday	Unknown
John L. Abramson	Oct. 31, 2016	Unknown	Wednesday	Navy
Arthur C. Ahlquist	Feb. 21, 2002	VFW 149	Monday	Army
Ronald D. Aich	Jan. 12, 2006	AL 600	Monday	Marines
Michael S. Anderson	July 31, 2011	VFW 5555	Friday	Army
Robert L. Anderson	June 3, 1989	VFW 1149	Tuesday	Army
Robert L. Anderson	July 30, 2009	AL 39	Wednesday	Army
Lloyd Antonson	Feb. 9, 2002	VFW 3877	Thursday	Army
Frederick W. Arcand	March 1, 2008	VFW 7555	Wednesday	Unknown
Jesse M. Arias	April 16, 2015	VFW 6690	Friday	Army
Harry J. Atkins, Sr.	May 8, 2010	AL 606	Tuesday	Army
Henry E. Austin	Nov. 18, 2002	VFW 6587	Monday	Unknown
Raymond R. Avoles	March 5, 1987	AL 449	Monday	Army Air
Basil J. Baker	May 6, 2002	VFW 4450	Thursday	Army
Meril C. Baker	June 15, 1989	VFW 9433	Wednesday	Army
Bernard B. Baird	Dec. 9, 2005	AL 533	Tuesday	Navy
Robert E. Baird	July 30, 1994	Ex-POW	Tuesday	Army
Gerald F. Barton	Nov. 23, 2014	AL 620	Thursday	Navy
Joseph Benkovics	Nov. 23, 1996	MOPH 5	Monday	Army Air
Roy A. Bennett	June 27, 1991	VFW 3877	Tuesday	Army
George K. Borgstrom	May 30, 2010	AL 600	Wednesday	Marines
Norbert Bosiger	Nov. 25, 1998	MOPH 268	Thursday	Army
Ladislaus J. Brabec	May 26, 2012	VFW 1296	Friday	Air Force
John V. Brletich	April 16, 2000	VFW 9625	Tuesday	Navy
John Buckho	Sept. 12, 1999	VFW 246	Wednesday	Unknown
Peter L. Buie	March 20, 2016	AL 542	Thursday	Air Force
Gerald L. Burger	Oct. 26, 2002	VFW 458	Thursday	Army
Phillip J. Carney	Dec. 12, 2012	VFW 9562	Monday	Army
Eugene M. Checkel	March 6, 2011	AL 542	Tuesday	Army
Dennis H. Christy	Aug. 9, 2008	VFW 1149	Monday	Army
Richard E. Clancy	Feb. 9, 1999	VFW 5907	Thursday	Army
Joseph F. Conley	July 21, 2010	AL 533	Tuesday	Air Force
Norman E. Cronquist	May 16, 1996	VFW 7555	Wednesday	Navy

Name	Date	Post	Day	Branch
Anthony C. Cuff	July 8, 2011	AL 440	Tuesday	Navy
Chester E. Danielson	Dec. 25, 2004	VFW 8752	Friday	Army
Frank J. DeMay	Sept. 10, 1996	AL 435	Tuesday	Army
Vernon Devine	July 8, 2004	VFW 1635	Wednesday	Coast Guard
John M. Doiron	Nov. 19, 1982	VFW 8217	Wednesday	Army
Thomas H. Dougherty	Feb. 13, 1991	AL 566	Monday	Army
Robert E. Drysdale	Dec. 23, 2011	AL 190	Monday	Army
Rolland J. Duff	May 7, 1995	VFW 1149	Monday	Army
Jerry A. Durheim	Dec. 24, 2013	DAV 39	Thursday	Marines
Lester A. Durose	Dec. 31, 2007	VFW 7555	Wednesday	Army
James E. Eddleston	Nov. 19, 1994	VFW 7555	Tuesday	Army Air
Gerald E. Eide	April 22, 1991	Unknown	Tuesday	Army
Russell V. Ek	July 23, 2010	VFW 7555	Tuesday	Army
Clayton Ekdahl	Oct. 14, 2004	VFW 4210	Friday	Army Air
Hubert L. Evans	June 30, 1993	VFW 1149	Monday	Army
Carl A. Falkowski, Sr.	Dec. 18, 2010	MOPH 5	Tuesday	Army
Samuel Faulk	Aug. 22, 1994	DAV 2	Tuesday	Army
Peter C. Feist	Oct. 25, 2011	VFW 8217	Tuesday	Air Force
Gilbert J. Fernandez	Feb. 15, 2009	AL 577	Thursday	Army
Walter J. Fick	Jan. 1, 2001	VFW 4450	Thursday	Army
Charles S. Fouzie	April 17, 1994	VFW 5630	Mon/Fri	Army Air
LeRoy P. Fran	March 11, 2009	VFW 5555	Tue/Fri	Marines
Robert W. Freas	Oct. 8, 1981	VFW 5907	Thursday	Navy
Wesley E. Fry	Dec. 24, 2001	AL 577	Tuesday	Marines
Phillip T. Garcia, Sr.	Aug. 20, 2005	KWV CH1	Monday	Army
James R. Gerber	Sept. 1, 2014	AL 102	Friday	Army
Martin J. Gilmore	March 19, 1990	VFW 5462	Wednesday	Army
Russell R. Green	Aug. 24, 2010	VFW 178	Tuesday	Marines
Albert G. Grenz	March 18, 1999	VFW 7555	Tuesday	Marines
Harold E. Gustafson	Nov. 25, 1994	DAV 1	Tuesday	Unknown
Ella M. Gustavson	Dec. 1, 1990	AL 435	Tuesday	Unknown
William M. Gutenkauf	Jan. 8, 2006	VFW 1852	Friday	Navy
Dean S. Hamre	Dec. 24, 1994	Army	Monday	Army

Name	Date	Post	Day	Branch
Wilfred A. Hanggi	April 24, 1984	VFW 5907	Thursday	Army
Danny J. Hannan	Nov. 21, 2000	VFW 6210	Monday	Navy
Kenneth E. Hardy	Feb. 28, 2013	AL 650	Thursday	Army
Wilmer W. Harris	Sept. 10, 2016	Unknown	Friday	Navy
Donn D. Hayes	Aug. 4, 2006	VFW 1782	Thursday	Marines
Hugh B. Heckel	May 19, 2015	VFW 1782	Tuesday	Army
Glenn O. Hendrickson	July 20, 1996	VFW 1149	Wednesday	Army
William W. Henninger	April 1, 2012	DAV 2	Thursday	Army
Wallace J. Herron	Feb. 8, 2007	VFW 7555	Tuesday	Navy
Morris D. Humphreys	March 29, 2011	AL 449	Thursday	Navy
John O. Imholte	March 20, 2014	VFW 7555	Wed/Thu	Army
Robert O. Imholte	Aug. 10, 2002	F.R.A.	Monday	Navy
Lloyd B. Isaacson	March 22, 1985	VFW 5555	Tuesday	Unknown
Michael P. Ivers	Aug. 22, 2005	AL 303	Wednesday	Navy
Lloyd J. Jackson	Feb. 17, 2007	VFW 5907	Thursday	Army
Joseph N. Jaspar	Dec. 6, 1996	VFW 5907	Thursday	Navy
Alois F. Jelinek	Oct. 10, 2009	VFW 6845	Friday	Navy
Kenneth L. Johnson	March 9, 2008	VFW 458	Thursday	Army
Larry Lee Johnson	July 3, 201	AL 172	Tue/Thu	Army
August F. Joubert	Dec. 21, 2016	Unknown	Thursday	Army
Burke W. Joyce, Jr.	April 23, 2007	VFW 6587	Monday	Navy
Donald W. Jurgs	March 11, 2001	MOPH	Thursday	Army
Edward A. Kalinoski	Jan. 14, 1992	Unknown	Unknown	Navy
Carl G. Karsten	Feb. 28, 2011	MCL	Friday	Marines
Aloysius P. Kapala	June 11, 1989	VFW 7555	Wednesday	Unknown
Paul Kingman	July 26, 2014	VFW 7051	Monday	Army
Edward J. Kirby	June 5, 2006	VFW 1635	Wednesday	Army
Donald A. Kirst	Dec. 26, 2006	VFW 8217	Thursday	Navy
James F. Lang	Dec. 14, 2007	VFW 458	Friday	Army
Daniel Langerbone	June 29, 1987	VFW 217	Wednesday	Army
Robert E. Larson	Jan. 31, 2001	VFW 1149	Monday	Army

Name	Date	Post	Day	Branch
John LaVaque	May 29, 2002	VFW 3877	Wednesday	Navy
Albert A. LaVansky	June 6, 2003	AL 533	Tues./Friday	Navy
Melvin P. Layman	Oct. 8, 2001	VFW 5555	Mon/Tue	Army
Glenn A. Lee	Jan. 26, 2013	VFW 458	Tuesday	Army
John H. Lloyd	Dec. 1, 1994	AL 411	Thursday	Air Force
Edward F. Loney	Oct. 2, 1997	VFW 5907	Wednesday	Marines
James R. Long	June 30, 1990	MOPH 5	Th/Friday	Army
Joseph F. Loss	Sept. 25, 2005	VFW 7555	Wednesday	Navy
Clarence A. Madsen	Sept. 2, 2006	VFW 6845	Wednesday	Army
Arnold V. Malaske	Dec. 9, 2012	VFW 7555	Wednesday	Army Air
Jack A. Martens	March 27, 2013	VFW	Unknown	Army
John A. Matschi	June 23, 2017	VFW 5555	Tuesday	Army
Jerome J. McFadden	July 11, 1998	VFW 5907	Thursday	Army
Robert L McGuir	Jan. 13, 1994	VFW 4393	Mon/Tue	Marines
Bernard R. Melter	Nov. 29, 2015	VFW 4452	Tuesday	Marines
Walter Michelson	Dec. 13, 2012	AL 251	Monday	Army Air
Earl F. Miller	Sept. 25, 2011	DAV	Thursday	Army Air
Robert C. Miller	April 21, 1999	VFW 5907	Thursday	Air Force
Kenneth R. Mishler	April 23, 1998	MOPH 268	Tue/Th	Army
William Morgan-Ryan	Nov. 10, 1982	M.C.L.	Friday	Marines
Donald C. Mueller	Nov. 27, 1982	VFW 246	Monday	Army
Frank J. Murawski	Nov. 11, 2007	VFW 6845	Friday	Navy
John E. Nelson	March 6, 1982	VFW 1296	Wednesday	Army
Kenneth E. Nelson	Jan. 1, 2002	VFW 5555	Wednesday	Air Force
Rudolph A. Nessman	Oct. 12, 2001	VFW 363	Monday	Army
Joseph J. Nicosia	Feb. 11, 1984	MOPH 5	Monday	Army
David P. Niles	July 12, 2010	AL 334	Monday	Navy
Martin J. O'Donnell	Aug. 31, 1990	AL 474	Tuesday	Navy
Norwood G. Olsen	Nov. 23, 1993	VFW 1149	Friday	Army
John L. O'Neill, Jr.	May 30, 2006	VFW 6845	Monday	Marines
Roy H. Opine	Dec. 29, 1987	AL 310	Tuesday	Army
Edwin J. Ostlund	Jan. 20, 2015	VFW 217	Monday	Navy/Marines

Name	Date	Post	Day	Branch
Richard T. O'Toole	Aug. 27, 2011	MER MAR	Tuesday	Mer. Marines
Norman Owens	Dec. 8, 2003	VFW 7555	Wednesday	Army
George R. Patton	April 21, 2009	AL 406	Monday	Navy
Norman F. Paul	July 18, 2011	AL 39	Tuesday	Navy
Oliver C. Pederson	Jan. 24, 1996	AL 435	Tuesday	Army
George W. Pesch	July 14, 1984	Unknown	Thursday	Army
Thomas V. Picha	Feb. 7, 2001	VFW 7555	Wednesday	Navy
Wayne A. Pickett	July 10, 2010	VFW 6587	Monday	Marines
Larry C. Phillips	Aug. 26, 2011	AL 102	Thursday	Army
Lawrence J. Pluta	Feb. 14, 1995	F.R.A.	Tuesday	Navy
John J. Possert	Feb. 24, 2007	VFW 1635	Wednesday	Navy
Craig R. Purdy	Aug. 9, 2001	VFW 7555	Tuesday	Army
Igor P. Razskazoff	Aug. 5, 1999	DAV 2	Thursday	Army
Robert W. Rice	June 21, 1997	VFW 5555	Friday	Army
Charles S. Rieland	May 28, 2014	Al 377	Thursday	Army
Clarence A. Roban	Nov. 18, 2009	VFW 7555	Thursday	Navy
Henry B. Robotnik	May 22, 2002	VFW 7555	Tuesday	Army Air
Martin J. Roeser	Feb. 24, 1993	VFW 1635	Wednesday	Navy
Richard D. Roland	Aug. 29, 2003	VFW 7555	Wednesday	Navy
Edward E. Rosander	Nov. 20, 1983	VFW 4160	Thursday	Army
David G. Rud	Jan. 22, 2012	AL 406	Monday	Army
Clarence F. Sassor	Nov. 17, 1995	VFW 458	Mon/Th/Fri	Army Air
Albert P. Schaeppi	March 22, 2000	VFW 5907	Thursday	Army
Joseph C. Schmidt	Feb. 16, 2004	VFW 1350	Thursday	Army
Dutch Schmiedeberg	June 9, 2012	VFW 7555	Wednesday	Air Force
Melvin S. Schofield	July 3, 2009	VFW 4462	Friday	Marines
Sherman T. Schultz	Oct. 12, 1998	VFW 7555	Mon/Fri	Army Air
Joseph F. Selbitschka	June 26, 1996	VFW 6845	Friday	Army Air
Joseph F. Serpico	July 27, 1997	VFW 3877	Thursday	Navy
Charles D. Sikonia	Aug. 23, 2016	VFW 5907	Thursday	Army
James N. Skiff	Dec. 2, 2014	AL 251	Wednesday	Army
Donald E. Skyberg	July 18, 2000	VFW 7555	Tuesday	Navy
Peter J. Slonski	Aug. 7, 1982	VFW 5555	Wednesday	Unknown
Gerald A. Smith	July 10, 2011	VFW 295	Monday	Army

Name	Date	Post	Day	Branch
John Smith	Dec. 29, 2002	VFW 8752	Friday	Army
Harold O. Stener	June 25, 2017	AL 533	Tuesday	Army
Richard A. Stevens, Sr.	Jan. 2, 2014	VFW 259	Wednesday	Navy
James D. Stewart	Oct. 4, 1994	E.R.A.	Tuesday	Navy
Leander P. Stoffel	Sept. 24, 2002	VFW 3877	Wednesday	Navy
George S. Stone	Oct. 20, 1998	VFW 9625	Tuesday	Army
John L. Stone	Nov. 9, 2009	VFW 246	Friday	Army
Calvin L. Sullivan	April 20, 2008	AL 433	Tuesday	Navy
William E. Sundet	Dec. 17, 1998	VFW 5555	Tuesday	Unknown
Robert B. Swanson	Dec. 30, 1998	VFW 5907	Friday	Navy
Glenn E. Swenningsen	April 26, 1998	DAV 2	Thursday	Navy
Frank N. Thill	Feb. 16, 1994	VFW 6587	Monday	Navy
Irving F. Thompson	Sept. 8, 2003	AL 47	Friday	Coast Guard
Michael Thompson	March 4, 2013	AL 586	Monday	Coast Guard
Kenneth K. Tjosvold	Feb. 25, 1998	VFW 6587	Mon/Fr	Navy
Guy V. Tomasino	Dec. 4, 2001	VFW 6210	Monday	Army
George J. Turnbull	Jan. 30, 1990	VFW 9562	Monday	Army
Hugh E. Vatsatk	Sept. 4, 2011	VFW 1296	Mon/Fri.	Marines
Michael Volinsky	April 25, 1983	VFW 458	Wednesday	Army
Neville E. Wagoner	July 1, 1996	VFW 5907	Tuesday	Army
Clemence J. Waldera	April 18, 2000	DAV 2	Thursday	Army
Henry G. Weber	March 25, 1992	DAV 2	Thursday	Navy
Wilfred J. Weber	Oct. 5, 1997	VFW 1149	Tuesday	Army Air
Fred G. Welch	June 21, 2003	Unknown	Unknown	Army
John A. Wilkus	June 18, 2000	VFW 6845	Wed.	Coast Guard
Lawrence J. Wilson	Feb. 26, 2003	DAV 2	Tuesday	Unknown
Daniel O. Winsjansen	Sept. 30, 2009	AL 168	Wednesday	Air Force
Alton Wold	Sept. 3, 1996	VFW 1635	Thursday	Army
Charles A. Wolford	Nov. 11, 2009	VFW 1296	Tuesday	Army
William H. Wright	April 17, 1983	MOPH 5	Charter	Army
Gordon O. Young	May 3, 2006	Unknown	Thursday	Army
Erwin E. Zimmer	Nov. 6, 2016	AL 1776	Tuesday	Navy

Addendum

PLEDGE OF ALLEGIANCE

I pledge allegiance to the flag of the United States of America, and to the republic for which it stands, one nation under God, indivisible, with liberty and justice for all.

FLAG DISPLAY DAYS

New Year's Day – January 1
Inauguration Day (Presidential) – January 20
Martin Luther King, Jr., Day – (3rd Monday of January)
Lincoln's Birthday – February 12
Presidents' Day – 3rd Monday of February
Easter Sunday – (variable)
Mother's Day – 2nd Sunday in May
*Peace Officer's Memorial Day – May 15
Armed Forces Day – 3rd Saturday in May
*Memorial Day – last Monday in May
Flag Day – June 14
Father's Day – 3rd Sunday in June
Independence Day – July 4
National Korean War Veterans Armistice Day – July 27
Labor Day – 1st Monday in September
*Patriot Day/National Day of Service and Remembrance – Sept. 11
POW/MIA Recognition Day – 3rd Friday in September
Constitution and Citizenship Day – Sept. 17
Columbus Day – 2nd Monday in October
Navy Day – October 27
Veterans' Day – November 11
Thanksgiving Day – 4th Thursday in November
*Pearl Harbor Remembrance Day – December 7
Christmas Day – December 25

* flag at half-staff

Note: Other such "flag" days may be proclaimed by the President of the United States, the birthdays of states (dates of admission—Minnesota, May 11), and state holidays.

FLAG ETIQUETTE
Standards of Respect

The Flag Code, which formalizes and unifies the traditional ways in which we give respect to the flag, also contains specific instructions on how the flag is not to be used. They are:

The flag should never be dipped to any person or thing. It is flown upside down only as a distress signal or during an emergency.

The flag should not be used as a drapery, or for covering a speaker desk, draping a platform, or for any decoration in general. Bunting of blue, white, and red stripes is available for these purposes. The blue stripe of the bunting should be on top.

The flag should never be used for any advertising purpose. It should not be embroidered, printed, or otherwise impressed on such articles as cushions, handkerchiefs, napkins, boxes, or anything intended to be discarded after temporary use. Advertising signs should be attached to the staff or halyard.

The flag should not be used as clothing or part of a costume, or athletic uniform, except that a flag patch may be used on the uniform of military personnel, fireman, policeman, and members of patriotic organizations.

The flag should never have placed on it, or attached to it, any mark, insignia, letter, word, number, figure, or drawing of any kind.

The flag should never be used us a receptacle for receiving, holding, carrying, or delivering anything.

The flag should not be displayed during inclement weather, except when an all-weather flag is being utilized.

The flag should never be stored where it might get dirty.

The flag should not be fastened or tied back; always allow it to fall free.

When the flag is lowered, no part of it should touch the ground or any other object; it should be received by waiting hands and arms. To store the flag, it should be folded neatly and ceremoniously. The flag should be cleaned and mended when necessary.

FLAG DISPOSAL

When a flag is so worn it is no longer fit to serve as a symbol of our country, it should be destroyed by burning in a dignified manner (Note: Most American Legion posts regularly conduct a dignified flag-burning ceremony on Flag Day, June 14). Many Cub Scout, Boy Scout, and Girl Scout troops retire flags regularly, as well.

The flag should be folded in its customary manner

It is important that the fire be fairly large and of sufficient intensity to ensure complete burning of the flag.

Place the flag on the fire.

The individual(s) can come to attention, salute the flag, recite the Pledge of Allegiance, and have a brief period of silent reflection.

After the flag is completely consumed, the fire should then be safely extinguished and the ashes buried.

Please make sure you are conforming to fire codes and ordinances in your area.

Displaying the Flag Outdoors

When the flag is displayed from a staff projecting from a window, balcony, or building, the union should be at the peak of the staff unless the flag is at half-staff. When it is displayed from the same flagpole with another flag—of a state, community, society, or Scout unit—the flag of the United States must always be at the top except that the church pennant may be flown above the flag during church services for Navy personnel when conducted by a Navy chaplain on a ship at sea.

When the flag is displayed over a street, it should be hung vertically, with the union to the north or east. If the flag is suspended over a sidewalk, the flag's union should be farthest from the building.

When flown with flags of states, communities, or societies on separate flagpoles that are of the same height and in a straight line, the U.S. flag is always placed in the position of honor—to its own right. The other flags may be smaller but none may be larger. No other flag ever should be placed above it. The flag of the United States is always the first flag raised and the last lowered. When flown with the national banner of other countries, each flag must be displayed from a separate pole of the same height. Each flag should be the same size. They should be raised and lowered simultaneously. The flag of one nation may not be displayed above that of another nation.

Raising and Lowering the Flag

The flag should be raised briskly and lowered slowly and ceremoniously. Ordinarily, it should be displayed only between sunrise and sunset. It should be illuminated if displayed at night. The flag of the United States is saluted as it is hoisted and lowered. The salute is held until the flag is unsnapped from the halyard or though the last note of music, whichever is longest.

DISPLAYING THE FLAG INDOORS

When on display, the flag is accorded the place of honor, always positioned to its own right. Place it to the right of the speaker or staging area or sanctuary. Other flags should be to the left. The flag of the United States should be at the center and at the highest point of the group when a number of flags of states, localities, or societies are grouped for display. When one flag is used with the U.S. flag and the staffs are crossed, the flag of the United States is placed on its own right with its staff in front of the other flag. When displaying the flag against a wall, vertically or horizontally, the flag's union (stars) should be at the top, to the flag's own right, and to the observer's left.

PARADING AND SALUTING THE FLAG

When carried in a procession, the flag should be to the right of the marchers. When other flags are carried, the flag of the United States may be centered in front of the others or carried to their right. When the flag passes in a procession, or when it is hoisted or lowered, all should face the flag and salute.

THE SALUTE

To salute, all persons come to attention. Those in uniform give the appropriate formal salute. Citizens not in uniform salute by placing their right hand over the heart, and men with head cover should remove it and hold it to the left shoulder, hand over the heart. Members of organizations in formation salute upon command of the person in charge.

THE PLEDGE OF ALLEGIANCE
AND NATIONAL ANTHEM

The Pledge of Allegiance should be rendered by standing at attention, facing the flag, and saluting. When the national anthem is played or sung, citizens should stand at attention and salute at the first note and hold the salute through the last note. The salute is directed to the flag, if displayed, otherwise to the music.

THE FLAG IN MOURNING

To place the flag at half-staff, hoist it to the peak for an instant and lower it to a position halfway between the top and bottom of the staff. The flag is to be raised again to the peak for a moment before it is lowered. On Memorial Day, the flag is displayed at half-staff until noon and at full staff from noon to sunset. The flag is to be flown at half-staff in mourning for designated, principal government leaders and upon presidential or gubernatorial order. When used to cover a casket, the flag should be placed with the union at the head and over the left shoulder. It should not be lowered into the grave.

THE RIFLE SQUAD

By Lois Stodieck (member of VFW 1296 Ladies Auxiliary)

We stand here on this hallowed ground
With granite markers all around
Your friends and family gather near
They do not see us through their tears
And when the final words are said
We raise our guns above our heads
The morning sun is climbing higher
Our captain tells us when to fire
Although we fire seven guns
Our timing makes it seem like one
We stand together straight and tall
We listen to the bugle call
We watch them fold your country's flag
We turn and slowly walk away
But we will shoot again some day
We also know our time will come
And we will join you one by one
We'll march beside you as before
But in a place where there's no war
So rest in peace our comrade friend
Because we know it's not the end

About the Author

Jim Hoey was born and raised in Taconite, Minnesota, and graduated from Greenway High School and St. Mary's University in Winona. He spent 34 years as a secondary social studies teacher (American history, political science, and geography) in Shakopee and Farmington. He was proud to emphasize civic-minded behavior and the importance of patriotism to his students and vividly recalls his first observation of the Memorial Rifle Squad at Fort Snelling in January of 1982, when a friend's father was buried on a bitterly cold day.

Hoey published his first book, *Minnesota Twins Trivia*, in 2010 and has subsequently published *Puck Heaven (2011)*, on the Minnesota state boys high school hockey tournament, *Minnesota Vikings Trivia* (2013), and *Ike: Minnesota Hockey Icon* (2015) with former Edina hockey coach Willard Ikola. Each book has been published by Nodin Press. Hoey lives in Eagan with his wife, Ann, who was a pharmacist at the Veterans Affairs Medical Center for 30 years, and their son, Eddie.